Study Abroad and Immigration 101

Ashwin

ISBN: 978-969-40-9276-8

Dedication

This book is dedicated to all its readers, encompassing students, parents, consultants, education providers, and prospective migrants who share the common aspiration of making the dream of moving abroad a reality. Whether you're seeking motivation to study overseas or pursuing immigration intentions, this dedication is for you.

I genuinely hope that the information contained within these pages serves as a guiding light on your journey. For there is nothing more fulfilling than the pursuit of making not only your life but also the lives of your loved ones truly beautiful.

Acknowledgment

I would like to dedicate this book to my mother, Jamna, and my father, Hasmukh, who have given me endless and selfless love. To my dear mom, a lovely lady filled with boundless love for her child, I dedicate my work to you and want you to know that your little boy has grown up. To my dad, a man brimming with wisdom, I hope to hear you say that you are proud of me.

To my wife, Meeta, thank you for always supporting my extra hours in business and loving me so well throughout all the phases of this hectic and wonderful life we share.

And to my pillars of strength: Drashti, Ankit, Vishwa, and our Chief Excel Officer, Aarav.

Table Of Contents

About the Author

Ashwin is an executive coach possessing over 33 years of experience in helping people and organizations become better at leading and accomplishing their missions. His background includes working with senior and junior-level directors and CEOs with the main aim of assisting them to deliver the best performance they can.

Ashwin has counseled over 36,093 people. His work revolves around collaborating with them and helping them deliver the performance they can by unlocking their true potential.

Ashwin has served and worked in leadership roles with various companies, with some notable names such as Real Value, Standard Chartered Bank, Citibank, Axis Bank, and more.

Preface

Welcome to the world of international education, a realm where students broaden their horizons, challenge their limits, and set forth on journeys that can be truly life-transforming. This book serves as your guiding light through this captivating adventure.

In an era defined by global connectivity and boundless opportunities, the idea of studying abroad has become a beacon of hope for countless individuals seeking not just an education but an experience that shapes their future. As you turn the pages of this book, you'll encounter the intricate details of international education.

From the bustling campuses of American universities to the serene classrooms of Japanese institutions, each chapter unveils a checklist tailored to the unique experience of studying in a specific country.

Studying abroad is more than just acquiring a degree; it's an adventure of self-discovery, cultural appreciation, and personal growth. As you navigate the chapters within, remember that this book is not just a resource but your trusted companion. It will serve as a practical and informative guide, equipping you with the knowledge and inspiration needed to embark on this life-altering journey.

So, fasten your seatbelts, open your minds, and get ready to explore the world through education. Your journey begins here, and it's bound to be one of the most exciting and transformative experiences of your life.

Chapter 1

Getting Started: Why Study Abroad

Gaining access to knowledge or studying, in general, has been around for as long as one can possibly remember. Studying or learning is perhaps as old as time in several cases. However, have you ever wondered how the concept of studying abroad or international education came to be in the first place?

The traces of international studies can take us as far back as 1190 CE when Emo of Friesland decided to travel from the Netherlands to study at Oxford University in England. This started a pavement for international exchange in Europe for the next 800 years.

Ever since the adventure that Emo of Friesland took, the concept of studying abroad is something that has become a lot more common than one might think. Almost every college student dreams of getting a higher education from prestigious universities around the world. Not just that, foreign universities or foreign exchange programs, along with other facilities, help the students come and study in their institutes.

The point here is that international education, or the idea of studying abroad, has become a lot more popular than one might think, and it is growing rapidly. It certainly is something that does not seem to stop, either.

Sure, there was a time when COVID-19 got in the way of many plans for international education. But things are changing now, and this is perhaps the best time for anyone to study abroad.

The purpose of this book is simple: to help people study abroad. As discussed before, the whole idea of studying abroad has been around for ages now. However, people are finally opening more and more to it, and for all the good reasons. However, the one big hurdle with studying abroad is that many people get lost in the rut.

The rut is that they are not sure about where to get started and what to do first. Surely, studying abroad is not as easy as getting admitted into your local college or university as there are several tests involved in the process that are mandatory for a student before they even begin.

This tedious process alone discourages countless students from pursuing their dreams of studying abroad, especially when they look at the laundry list of things they need to look after to have a 'chance' at their dream university. Yes, a chance. Not even a confirmed admission.

However, what if I tell you that the entirety of this process is a lot easier than you might have thought? You do not need to go through all the hoops, and you can study abroad. Don't worry; there is no shortcut being sold, but there are ways that you can make your dream of studying abroad a lot easier.

At www.careerslead.com, https://ieltsnpte.com/, and Kumardirect.com, we bring you a one-stop-shop solution for your dream of studying abroad in any country you wish to emigrate to. We pride ourselves on providing an expert team with access to a great personality testing system for everyone.

The key here is accessibility, as it has become essential for everyone; everyone should be able to benefit from having an insight about themselves.

There are options for online and face-to-face counseling that can be used for both aptitude and personality tests.

The goal is to ensure that all the students trying their best to get into their favorite universities or college have the chance to do so and that too, without the need to jump through countless unnecessary hoops.

With the business, the target is simple: we want to make international education a reality for everyone.

Moving Abroad and Making Your Life Easy.

It is safe to say that the whole process of moving abroad is challenging for many people. However, we are here to make things easier for everyone planning to move overseas.

How do we do that? We are here to help you with your studies abroad, migration, and the whole process of working abroad.

We all have experienced going to our local schools and colleges, and most of us have also experienced going to other countries for our studies. It is always the latter that fascinates people the most.

One of the greatest mantras that can help you through this process is,

"You are not a tree."

This is something you should keep in mind before you decide to move abroad. No situation is permanent. If you're unhappy with your new city, job, or school, or if you feel like the place has nothing to offer, change the setting. None of this is permanent, and the worst thing you could do for yourself is think you must 'put up' in a bad situation. You can find a different place or move back home until you find the right opportunity that suits you. Living abroad is a choice, not a right. There is no point in making that change in your lifestyle if you're unhappy with it.

Make the most of your situation in a new city and return home with your head held high.

It is obvious that moving abroad through proper channels is just half the fight. The thing that really makes things difficult for everyone refers to finding the program that you are good at.

Thankfully, we are here to help everyone find the right footing so they can ensure they do it the right way.

How Can One Migrate Abroad?

Moving abroad can seem like a daunting task. However, one can take a few paths to make things easier for them.

- People can migrate through tier work by having a work visa, finding the right opportunities, and then going forward.
- Migrating through study is another excellent idea for those who are looking to study as well.
- Permanent residency is something that most people look towards. Thankfully, countries like Australia or Canada offer PR visas to those who qualify, as do other countries. You can always check the list.
- Last but not least, migration through investment and entrepreneurship is another way. A lot of developed and progressive countries invest in potential investors, which is an excellent way of migrating.

It surely is an intimidating task, but with the proper guidance that we are here to provide you with, things will make sense for you to move to a different country and study as much as you want

If you are confused about things like financial requirements, the visa process, as well as all the necessary preparations that you will need to make, we are here to help you with that.

Benefits of Studying Abroad

But why exactly should you study abroad? This question has been central for almost everyone for the longest time possible. You can get countless advantages from studying abroad, and we will take a stroll and look at all of them.

The benefits are, of course, subjective. Still, most people will more than easily be able to understand and relate to them as they would want the same for themselves.

The Exposure That Comes

Although this is not something everyone will want, the exposure that comes with studying abroad is something that you cannot simply deny or overlook. The biggest benefit here is that you are exploring the world and different cultures.

You are getting the chance to experience a new country with many customs activities, along with other previously uncharted terrains. Sure, at some point, it would almost sound like it is rudimentary, but the more you explore and learn, the better you feel about being in a new country.

Another great thing is that visiting neighboring countries becomes a lot easier with studying abroad. For instance, if you are studying in France, you will have the opportunity to explore various parts of not just Europe without a hassle but also North African countries.

Quality Education

Now, this one is something that should be a no-brainer for anyone who is trying to study abroad. Quality education is something that most people want to get their hands on. I am not saying that local formal education is not good enough. However, when studying abroad, you get to learn how different cultures incorporate education.

You will get the chance to immerse yourself in an educational system that is inherently different than the one that you are used to. It will be challenging in the beginning, but you will get to experience a lot more. As a result, you will grow exponentially academically and intellectually.

You will also get the chance to learn new languages and hone your skills. Of course, as an English speaker, you might want to stay reserved for that language. However, sooner or later, you will realize that having the ability to speak or at least understand multiple languages is always better.

New Culture, New People

Another thing that I often tell people, especially students, when it comes to studying abroad is that it is an excellent choice for getting familiar with a new culture and people. Do not look at your chance of studying abroad as something you are doing for education. Think of it as a holiday, and you will realize how quickly the experience changes.

You will get to immerse yourself in an entirely new culture and be with people from all parts of the world. For anyone who wants to understand the world around them and its inhabitants in a better way, studying abroad is definitely something that one needs to look into.

Career Opportunities

Aside from getting access to a great education, another great thing about studying abroad is that you get access to many career opportunities. Most of us tend to go for a better education to get into better careers, which is exactly what studying abroad will provide you with.

No matter the field you are pursuing, a shot at a good career is always something that comes with being in institutes that are recognized the world over.

Personal Growth

For a lot of us, personal growth matters a lot. After all, if we don't grow as people, we will not be able to process things or understand life as it should be understood. Living in a strange land with strangers will help us understand how independence works.

This is an excellent opportunity for anyone looking to get the development on their part and grow into better people. It will not be easy in the beginning, but things are seldom easy when they guarantee great results.

Studying abroad comes with many benefits. However, convincing students to get up and leave the comfort of their homes is not easy without strong backing to the statements made.

Now, discussing studying abroad can happen at three levels. You can choose to study abroad in school, during undergraduate studies, or after graduating.

This is another thing that confuses most of the students, and we will make it simpler for you by telling you about the advantages of studying abroad as undergraduate and graduate students.

The purpose here is to help you develop a better understanding so you do not get lost trying to figure out what you should be doing as an aspiring international student.

Benefits of Studying Abroad for School Students

Perhaps the most exposure a person can get is if they decide to study abroad as a school student. This decision is not entirely autonomous because convincing your parents is a huge part of the conversation.

However, there are a handful of benefits that you can get from studying abroad, and you can look at them below.

New Perspective

Studying abroad is excellent for school students because it is a great way of getting access to new perspectives.

Most school students are still in that phase where their thoughts and perspectives are slowly being formulated, and exposure to an international education system and culture can completely and dramatically overhaul their personalities.

Finding Your Calling

Another benefit you can get from studying abroad as a school student is that it helps many people find their calling.

This means that if you have been trying to find your identity, what you are, or what you are good at, studying abroad in school is an excellent way because you can easily see that.

Many people get into arts, sports, or anything they are good at. The school they are studying in has encouraged them to get better at that specific part of life.

Building New Relations

Another thing that I believe is great about studying abroad in a school is that it helps you build excellent relationships. The friends and people you meet in school can be the closest allies for all the right reasons.

The reason behind that is that during that age, almost everyone you meet who is away from their home is vulnerable and has to face the world in more than one way. During those years, things can get overwhelming.

That is why people tend to stick together, and the relationships that are formed during those years end up being around for the longest time.

Becoming Better Humans

One more thing I stand by when it comes to international education is that it allows us to become better human beings overall.

When you are abroad, you are exposed to all sorts of knowledge and information you will need to look into.

The more you learn from cultures around the world, the more you adapt and, sometimes, make compromises, as well.

The point is that international education at the school level can turn you into a human being that most people fail to become even after years of schooling.

Benefits of Studying Abroad for Undergraduate Students

The life of an undergrad student can be summed up in one word—adventurous. For many people, this is a new ushering into a lifestyle that is inherently different from what students are used to, and this is the time that can make or break a student.

Suppose you gear up and decide to spend your undergrad years abroad. In that case, the good news is that you will have many experiences that will help shape your life for the better and open more doors for you.

It Teaches You a Lot

Going abroad for a diploma or bachelor's degree is not easy for everyone. You are leaving the comfort of your home for two, three, to four years; this means removing yourself from a familiar environment and entering uncharted territory.

As a young person, you'll get to learn to handle many tasks that might have seemed simple to you before. For example, going through the steps to open a bank account, taking care of your money, buying groceries, paying utility bills, and much more.

If you are new to the country and do not speak their native language, it will be a unique experience for you. It will also not be easy, but in the end, it will help you become a better version of yourself.

A Great Way to Learn New Skills

The main point of studying abroad is the opportunity to learn new skills that you might have missed out on if you had chosen a different path. Being in an unfamiliar country, you'll need to get used to things like embracing different cultures and making friends with people worldwide.

These cross-cultural communication skills could feel like just a necessity to you at that point, but in the future, these are going to help you a lot, especially if you want to work in an international job market.

There is a lot to Learn.

You will be exposed to an entirely new educational system when you get an education abroad. This will allow you to pick and hone the one craft you are interested in. Undergraduate degrees are the root of how we progress in the future, and having a diverse choice is always better for those looking for their calling.

In addition to that, even the grading system is there. Therefore, you will get a whole host of new challenges that you will have to undertake to spend your time there and become a better student successfully.

A Great Way of Expanding the Network

Another benefit of studying internationally as an undergraduate student is that it is an excellent way of expanding your network. You will be meeting people from different corners of the world. You will develop meaningful relationships with them that can easily stand the test of time.

This is an excellent choice for all undergrads to expand their network. The same network will help them in the future as they enter the market for jobs or further studies, for that matter.

Traveling, Cultures, Traditions, and Languages

When studying abroad as an undergrad student, you are keener to learn about things you otherwise might not pay much attention to.

Traveling is a huge part of the experience as you might have to go to different cities or locales to learn more about the places and their history.

Similarly, you will be exposed to new cultures and traditions. While it might seem difficult to adapt initially, it all comes together the more you spend time there. Remember, it is always better to keep your horizons open so you do not isolate yourself.

Last but not least, the whole idea of learning new languages and understanding the importance of languages while being an undergrad student is a thrilling experience and a half. It will take time, but it will be worth it.

How Graduate-Level Students Can Benefit from Studying Abroad

Life often puts us in a situation where we have to settle for local education rather than going abroad for our undergrad studies. However, that does not mean not trying again and going abroad for our graduation-level studies because many, many.

Now, a lot of students think that just because they missed their chance to go abroad in their undergrad, they cannot do that at a graduate level. That is not true, as several universities offer graduate-level options to study internationally. If you want to study abroad, I would highly suggest that you read on and get to know more.

1. You Get to Experience New Teaching Styles

Experiencing various teaching styles is always a great experience for everyone. When studying abroad at an undergrad or graduate level, you get to experience different teaching styles.

You could experience a teacher-centric style where the professor acts as the authority, and most lectures are a one-way presentation with a focus on a set of rules.

There are also teaching methods where the professors allow the students to self-learn. Then, there are cases when the professors assign lab activities and give students various projects that help them stay engaged and learn new things along the way.

The point here is that there are various learning methods, and if you are trying to get better at learning through multiple means, this is an excellent way as it hones your craft even further.

2. Shot at a Great Career

Another benefit graduates get from studying abroad is a chance at a great career. You get to find new places where you can work to impress your employers, especially with your ability to adapt to various situations and environments.

Most employers out there are always looking for graduates who have had international exposure and possess transferrable skills. Even at a graduate level, you are getting an excellent choice of making a career as long as you have your mind set on it.

3. Confidence Development and Personal Growth

Confidence development and personal growth are something that is never going to stop. Even if you missed your shot at international studies as an undergrad, you can still indulge in developing your confidence and growing as a person.

When studying abroad, you can develop your skills in various factors such as leadership, communication, and cross-cultural awareness. All of these combined will help you grow as a person and boost your confidence at the same time.

4. Meeting New People and Learning New Things

You are never too old to meet new people and learn new things. Even if you are going abroad for studies as a graduate, you are still getting a shot at meeting new people and learning a heap of new things that are not just going to form life experiences for you but will also help you become better at communication, understanding, and relating to people.

When you are in uncharted territory, the world opens to you, and everything is out there for you to reach out.

When it comes to getting admissions to colleges abroad and studying there, it would help if you went through specific tests as they are basic requirements that must be fulfilled. This often becomes a roadblock for many students as they believe these will only hinder their plans.

These 'tests' only sound challenging when you look at their names; otherwise, you are just looking at something easy to understand.

Below, you will find a list of tests you might have to take depending on your area of study and the university. Remember, not all tests are required, so you do not have to pass all of them.

- **IELTS**: IELTS, or the International English Language Testing System, is an international standardized English language proficiency test for non-native English speakers. The British Council, IELTS Australia, and Cambridge Assessment English manage IELTS. There are two IELTS tests available – IELTS Academic, which measures the level of English proficiency suitable for an academic environment, and IELTS General Training, which measures English proficiency in everyday context. The test assesses an individual's listening, reading, writing, and speaking skills.
- **TOEFL**: TOEFL, or Test of English as a Foreign Language, is a standardized test used to measure the English language ability of non-native speakers looking forward to enrolling in English-speaking institutes. The test is valid for over 11,000 universities spread across 190 countries. Like IELTS, TOEFL is also used to assess an individual's reading, writing, listening, and speaking ability.
- **PTE**: PTE or Pearson Test of English is a computer-based academic English test for non-native speakers looking to study abroad.
- **CAE**: CAE or Certificate in Advanced English is a test that often serves as an alternative to IELTS. It is managed by Cambridge ESOL and is accepted in nearly every university and college in the UK. It is also accepted in institutions in Australia as well as other countries. Like all the tests previously mentioned, this one also involves reading, writing, listening, and speaking.

In addition to the tests, there are some entrance tests that one might have to take depending on the program they choose.

- **SAT**: SAT is a standardized test widely used for college admissions in the United States. It is a multiple-choice test created and administered by the College Board. The test mainly looks at mathematical skills and evidence-based reading and writing, lasting 3 hours. The highest SAT score is 1,600, with 1,060 being the average.

- **ACT**: Similar to SAT, ACT is also a standardized test that is used for college admissions in the United States. The test covers four academic skills: English, mathematics, reading, and scientific reasoning. It also has writing as an optional section that some colleges require.

- **GRE**: GRE, or the Graduate Record Examinations, is another form of standardized test that is an admission requirement for several graduate schools in the United States as well as Canada, along with a few other countries. The test is essential for master's or doctoral degree programs, with the test being valid in over 160 countries worldwide. The test is 3 hours and 45 minutes long, with a 1-minute break after completing each section and a 10-minute break after the third section.

- **GMAT**: GMAT or Graduate Management Admission Test is a computer adaptive test to assess analytical, writing, quantitative, verbal, and reading skills in written English, and it is a prerequisite for graduate management programs such as MBA. The test is mainly there to assess an individual's critical thinking skills. Knowing how to reason through the provided information and analyze it allows for a great GMAT score.

Chapter 2:

How To Choose the Right Program for You

Preparations for major exams like engineering, CAT, GRE, MBA, GMAT, TOEFL, and civil service require a huge chunk of your time and money. You have to invest years into preparing for these life-changing tests. A typical top degree from India, IIT/IIM, requires two to three years of classes and practice and approximately two to three million rupees as an initial investment.

In the US, an MBA from a renowned university can cost up to $150,000. We make this massive investment because we trust our education will determine a bright future. We want the best for our careers, so we don't think twice about going the extra mile. As you are investing so much of your assets, you need to make the right decision about your chosen program.

If you want to study in Australia, the Department of Home Affairs recently released a beneficial report about the country's visa programs that you should be aware of. Roughly 230,000 student visas were granted between 2021 and 2022, but under 40 percent of those given were issued to students from leading countries as they were returning to Australia between November 2021 and May 2022. The statistics for issued student visas for various countries are as follows:

India	34,035
China	25,689
Nepal	18,889
Vietnam	7,172

Moreover, lodgments for student visas skyrocketed to 473,415 in 2018 and 2019, then dipped again to 262,633 in 2020 and 2021 because of the COVID-19 pandemic. However, applications for student visas saw a new high when they reached 314,388 in May 2022. If you are applying for a student visa, there are some important dates you have to keep in mind. According to current reports, Australia's government ends its fiscal year on 30th June, but Australia's borders were open for abroad students till 15th December 2021.

These dates were altered after an extended period of border closures due to the global pandemic. These statistics demonstrate the number of students traveling to Australia between December 2021 and May 2022.

Looking at China's statistics, we see a similar pattern in lodged student visa applications over the same period. Chinese students lodged 91,296 visa applications in 2018 and 2019, but the numbers plummeted to 52,041 in 2020 and 2021. They saw a slight high when they reached 55,601 in May 2022. The volume of student applications demonstrates only 60 percent of the volume of Chinese visa applications before the pandemic hit.

On the other hand, Indian applicants diverted back to sixty-four percent of the volume before COVID-19. The numbers fell from 89,868 in 2018 and 2019 to 57,635 in 2021 and 2022. The applications lodged by Nepalese students returned to ninety percent of the pre-pandemic levels, falling to 39,066 in 2021 and 2022 from 43,190 in 2018 and 2019. Furthermore, the government released details on international students' study and work rights after they entered the country.

Indian applications for master's programs in the U.S. increased by 36 percent in 2021 compared to 2019. The first-time enrolment of Indian students was up by 430%.

According to the revised laws, degree-level students will remain eligible for study work rights. However, non-degree students will be allowed to work after their studies and if their qualifications correspond with an occupation on the Green List. The categories on this list corroborate with shortages in labor market skills. Such students can only work in a career that the Green List supports.

According to New Zealand, this list contains 85 occupations. The government claims that the list will give a streamlined and prioritized map for finding a residency, incentivizing skilled healthcare providers, engineers, tech experts, and trade workers to move to the country permanently. Additionally, graduate students are eligible for three years of post-graduate employment in the country.

None of the abroad students would be allowed to apply for a second work permit because, according to the government, it will help reduce the time it takes for someone to work in New Zealand without applying for an Accredited Employer Work Visa, which requires the employer to check if a New Zealand citizen is available to carry out a particular occupation.

Moving to New Zealand for your studies will require extensive financial resources. Apart from the five thousand students under the "cohort 4" designation, international students must provide proof of additional funds to cover New Zealand accommodation costs. Moreover, higher education and English-speaking students will be required to prove ownership of assets worth NZD 20,000 annually. In contrast, primary and secondary students must show assets worth NZD17,000. Previous rules dictated that each level of study required NZD15,000 per year.

Additionally, international students will have to pay their full tuition fees for the first year of their studies upfront. They can pay for the first program they undertake if it is short, but it must be paid upfront. The students who wish to transfer into a work permit must show proof of funds worth NZD5,000. A survey showed that around three-quarters of agents agreed that student interest in New Zealand increased in the last two months as compared to interest in other countries.

More than half of the agents related to the statement "strongly agreed," this was a massive change from the statistics in October 2021, when 28 percent of the surveyed agents agreed that Australia had the upper hand against its competitors regarding international students. According to Navitas, Australia has significantly breached the gap between the UK and Canada in terms of international students.

Students from South and Southeast Asia have shown the most interest in Australia as a potential destination for higher education. Almost ninety percent of the agents in those regions claimed that student interest in international studies in Australia picked up significantly in the last two months. General Manager for Global Recruitment UPA Navitas, Neil Fitzroy, identified some significant causes for Australian educators attracting more international students than leading countries. Australia's mid-year intake experienced a substantial rise in international student travel to Australia to resume or start their studies.

The energy and thrill in campuses across the country will prove well for future admissions, as speculated by surveyed agents. Recent research confirmed that there was a shift in sentiment amongst international students. Higher than ninety-five percent of the adult population is fully vaccinated. With COVID precautionary protocols still in place, significant advancement in Australia's global market share can be seen across the education sector.

Moreover, the expansion across global markets will be led by categories for international students. This planned increment will be driven directly by higher caps in the "Federal High Skilled" group of international students. This category accommodates the applications of international graduates from Canadian institutions. The number of slots in this category will increase from 55,900, the current number of spaces available, to 111,500 in 2024. The immigration streams that will cater to this expansion are already in place for international graduates. Some programs you should look out for if you plan on studying in Canada are the Federal Skilled Worker Program, the Federal Skilled Trades Program, and the Canadian Experience Class.

The new immigration targets for the Canadian government take two important prioritize into account:

- Attracting the most talented students and workers to join the Canadian labor market
- Helping refugees (particularly from Afghanistan) to make a new, safer home in Canada.

Canada's Immigration Minister, Marc Miller, explained to CIC News that these revised laws balance the country's needs and international obligations. These laws focus on attracting skilled individuals who can contribute to the country's labor force and economy to tackle the onset of labor shortages. These implementations also recognize the significance of reuniting families and helping the world's most vulnerable populations through refugee accommodation.

Canada's goal remains to support its economic development through greater retention of newcomers in areas laden with economic, labor, and demographic hurdles. The country takes pride in its achievements so far and is open to welcoming more international students to become a potential top country of choice.

Furthermore, immigration plans in Canada are designed to promote maximum occupation. This means that immigration is vital for Canada's economy to prosper.

The Canadian government states that immigration accounts for approximately 100% of labor force growth. With five million Canadians expected to retire by the end of the decade, the ratio between worker and retiree will fall to 3:1. This development is a clear sign of the economic requirement for increased immigration. Additionally, the government announced a new stream of immigration last year, centered explicitly around international workers and students, specializing in sectors that suffer from skilled labor market gaps. While releasing the revised Temporary to Permanent Residence Stream (TR2PR) policy, Minister of Immigration, Refugees, and CitizenshipMarco Mendicino explained how the pandemic impacted the prominent and magnificent contributions of new arrivals in the country.

Such new policies will assist people who hold a temporary status as citizens to plan a concrete future in Canada, play an indispensable role in the country's economic recovery, and help the government rebuild. Canada's approach to international students is very welcoming. Regardless of their temporary status, their contributions to the economy and labor force are seen as prominent and lasting.

The main avenues for residency used by international students to become permanent citizens of Canada will add to more than half of the new permanent residents of the country. Now, Canadian immigration executives have cut back on some of the spaces available in the Express Entry stream to make room for students in the TR2PR stream. This is a progressive step to accommodate more international students deciding what they want to study and when to come to Canada. Another thing to note is that the TR2PR stream specifically focuses on certain sectors and occupations so that international students can choose specific occupations.

Additionally, the Provincial Nominee Program, a gateway for inviting more international students to migrate to Canada, will grow its spaces from 83,500 in 2022 to 93,000 in 2024. Regardless of favorable laws, the processing system for Canadian immigration can be slow and frustrating. Such delay and unpredictability create agitation amongst Canadian visa applicants who want permanent residency, which has been going on for a while now.

Canadim, a Canadian immigration law firm, explains that during the height of the COVID-19 pandemic, most of the IRCC, Immigration, Refugees, and Citizenship staff were inactive. IRCC was unsuccessful in finalizing permanent resident applications due to border and travel restrictions. The aftermath of the pandemic resulted in massive application backlogs. From October 2021, IRCC had about 1.8 million applications in backlog. A similar pattern can be seen in the total number of visas granted to international students.

The numbers started from a high point of 405,742 in 2018 and 2019, but visa grants fell to 232,750 in 2020 and 2021. They have reached 56 percent of pre-pandemic levels, with 228,150 visas granted in 2021 and 2022. From June 2022, there have been a total of 469,306 Canadian student visa holders globally, and around three-quarters of that number, 354,475 students, were present in Canada. A balance of 114,831 is currently based outside of the country. Students outside of Canada are eligible to travel if they are fully vaccinated.

Australian state governments, a group of eight representing research universities, and universities in Australia were looking to strengthen ties with India, the second largest source of international students in 2022, which was ahead of the upcoming February intake.

Between January and July 2023, the count of international students pursuing courses in Australia reached 710,893. This figure indicates a 34% change compared to the corresponding period in the previous year. It's important to note that this international student count is a head count, encompassing all students on a student visa during a specific reference period. Therefore, a student might be included in this count across multiple years if their course of study spans multiple years.

In addition to the head count, there are international student enrolments and commencements, which measure the educational activity undertaken by students on a student visa. Since students have the flexibility to enroll in multiple courses across different sectors during the reference period, the enrolment and commencement count will always exceed the student count.

Due to the mobility of students across providers and states, the total student count for Australia will not necessarily match the total for all states.

It's worth mentioning that during the COVID-19 pandemic, not all international students studying will physically be in Australia.

Furthermore, it's important to acknowledge that there was a transition period from a state-based registration system for education providers to a nationally recognized registration system. During this transition, there were cases where the study location for certain students couldn't be determined, and for these cases, a 'Multi-State' location was assigned.

The immigration reforms in New Zealand reflect its government's commitment to linking immigration to economic priorities to streamline the flow of low-skilled labor from the country.

International students who wish to study in the UK must get a student visa (Tier 4). This type of visa is available for full-time university students pursuing a degree in the UK. Students getting short-term or language courses cannot live in the UK with this visa. You can apply for a student visa if you're sixteen years or above. Moreover, having a licensed student sponsor's offer for a place would be best. You also need to have enough finances to support yourself and pay for your educational program. This amount varies depending on your situation. Additionally, international students are required to speak, read, write, and understand English.

You must look at a country's educational programs, financial requirements, visa processes, and attitude toward immigrants before you decide to move there for your studies. It is best to pick a country that offers permanent residency after your studies are completed.

According to the ICEF Survey, the cost of living is the most critical factor in international students' choice of destination.

Chapter 3:

How to Find the Right Kind of Funding Sources

Going abroad to study is an exceptional idea, but you might hesitate due to a big glaring issue: funding.

You might wonder why it's so difficult to find sufficient funding to support your dreams of high-quality education. For most students, studying in one of the world's leading countries is a hard-to-pass experience. However, the skyrocketing tuition fees, travel, and lodging costs stop them from pursuing this opportunity. Luckily, all is not lost. You can find the right scholarship programs that assist you in fulfilling funding requirements and minimizing student loans.

To pick the most suitable program, you must first identify why students face funding issues while applying abroad. The most prominent sector that eats up funding is the tuition fees of high-ranking universities. There is no doubt that state-of-the-art education costs a lot of money. Usually, the cost of tuition for international students exceeds the cost of tuition for domestic students. The average fee for undergraduate courses in the US is $26,000 to $35,000. If you're looking for postgraduate studies, the average is around $40,000 to $50,000.

You can fill out the Eligibility questionnaire to check if you are eligible for various scholarships. It will check in detail if you meet all of the eligibility criteria. The eligibility questionnaire will check t he following:

- In which country do you hold citizenship
- How long you have been living in your home country
- How much work experience do you have
- Whether we provide scholarships to your country

You must complete the eligibility questionnaire before you can apply for a Scholarship.

After tuition, the biggest obstacle for international students is high living expenses. The cost of living in most developed countries exceeds an international student's monthly budget by a long shot. Such expenses include food, accommodation, transport, and miscellaneous daily costs, which vary monthly and can quickly pile up. In Europe, the average monthly cost of living lies around €700 to €1000. Similarly, in the US, the price rises to new heights at an average monthly stipend of living of around $1200 to $1500. These numbers can be even higher if you choose to live in developed cities or business hubs like New York or Los Angeles.

In addition to living expenses, flights, and visa applications can empty an international student's pockets before they reach a new country. This expense is dependent mainly on the country you are going to. Some countries have costly tickets, especially for airfare. Now, if you decide to study in a developed country like the US, you need to add the cost of a student visa to your budget. The average price of a student visa for the USA is approximately $160.

Once you finally reach a new country with the hopes for a brighter future, you are hit with additional costs of academic materials, like books. You might not believe it, but textbooks can chip away at your funds. This cost varies with your courses, but some courses require you to purchase specific textbooks, and you might not have the funds for that. Another vital factor to consider is the rise of e-learning and the digitalization of education. Not all students have the money to purchase laptops or access printers for their assignments.

After identifying these problems, you can look for funding support that suits your specific situation. Several study-abroad programs support specific countries, and you can apply for them to finance your education. The trick to picking the most suitable program is knowing the scholarship policies for the country you are applying to.

The first option for funding is applying for financial aid. If you are a US citizen, you can apply for federal financial aid or federal student aid because you fit the eligibility criteria. This funding includes grants, loans, and work-study programs. Suppose you don't want to go through the public sector's route. In that case, you can apply for scholarships and grants from private organizations, foundations, or financial aid offices. As an international student, you can apply for international financial aid programs. However, the eligibility criteria for such programs can be restrictive.

You can apply for scholarships or international educational grants besides financial aid. Several institutions and organizations offer sufficient scholarship programs specified for international students who wish to study abroad. The best way to find these programs is by searching the internet or contacting your school's academic counselors. But, the most effective route is contacting the study-abroad offices, which can provide you with a detailed list of available scholarships and grant programs. Countries like the US, Australia, and the UK offer the best scholarship programs for international students.

Another effective route is taking out student loans for additional funding. Student loans are labeled as one of the most suitable financial tools for financing international education and its related expenses. Student loans offer several advantages, such as low and affordable interest rates, long repayment times, and deferred payment options. You can apply for student loans from government-funded institutions or private organizations. However, student loan debt becomes a huge issue after students graduate, and most people cannot pay off their entire debt during their lifetime.

The top scholarship programs that offer the most generous funding for abroad students are:

1. Fulbright Scholarships (USA)

The Fulbright Scholarship is a respected scholarship program that the US government funds. The scholarship is offered to non-US students worldwide who want to pursue a master's degree or PhD in the United States.

2. Chevening Scholarships (UK)

The Chevening Scholarship is a fully funded scholarship program offered to international students from over 160 countries who want to earn a master's degree in the United Kingdom. It is one of the world's most renowned and cut-throat scholarship programs.

3. Eiffel Excellence Scholarship Program (France)

If you plan to study in France, you may be eligible for the Eiffel Excellence Scholarship Program. This scholarship is curated for international students pursuing a master's degree or PhD in France. This scholarship looks for academic brilliance and cultural diversity.

4. DAAD Scholarships (Germany):

The DAAD scholarship is a government-funded scholarship program offered by Germany, and it is awarded to international students from all over the world who want to pursue an academic degree in Germany. It is one of the most popular and attainable scholarships for international students.

5. Emerging Leaders in the Americas Program

The Emerging Leaders in the Americas Program provides students from Latin America and the Caribbean with short-term exchange opportunities for study or research at Canadian post-secondary institutions.

6. Canada-CARICOM Skills Training for the Green Economy Scholarships

The Canada-CARICOM Skills Training for the Green Economy Scholarships provide students from the Caribbean Community (CARICOM) member states with short-term exchange opportunities at publicly funded Canadian colleges and institutes.

Apart from these, scholarship programs vary from country to country. Canada is one of the leading countries in the world in terms of education and scholarships. They have several programs that assist abroad students in finding suitable grants and scholarships. The government of Canada participates in international scholarship programs through Global Affairs Canada. They include international scholarships offered by Canadian governments, foreign governments, non-governmental organizations, and international organizations. The "Study in Canada Scholarships" provide abroad students in post-secondary institutions located in the new eligible countries/territories with short-term exchange program opportunities for study and research in Canadian post-secondary institutions at college, undergraduate, and graduate levels.

The Government of Ontario partnered up with WeRPN to create the BEGIN program. This program acts as a bridge between Personal Support Workers (PSWs) and Registered Practical Nurses (RPNs) to discover different professional pathways in Long-Term Care (LTC) and Home and Community Care (HCC). Suppose you're enrolled in a certified and accredited PSW-RPN or RPN-RN program. In that case, the BEGIN program will reimburse its participants through tuition grants. When you graduate, the program will open doors for you to connect with significant employment opportunities in Ontario's LTC and HCC sectors. Moreover, eligible PSWs can receive tuition reimbursement of up to $6,000 per year (maximum of $15,000). Additionally, eligible RPNs can receive tuition reimbursement of up to $10,000 per year (maximum of $30,000).

The Canada-CARICOM Skills Training for the Green Economy Scholarships also offers short-term exchange opportunities at publicly funded Canadian colleges and institutes for students from the Caribbean Community (CARICOM) member states. The Emerging Leaders in the Americas Program offers short-term exchange opportunities for study or research at Canadian post-secondary institutions for students from Latin America and the Caribbean.

Suppose you want to limit your search to Australia for higher studies. In that case, the Australia Awards is one of the most compelling scholarship programs. The Australia Awards encourage knowledge, educational networks, and lasting ties between Australia and its neighbors through the country's extensive scholarship programs. For 2022, the Department of Foreign Affairs and Trade (DFAT) offered 2,075 Australia Awards scholarships and short courses to individuals from 27 developing countries at an estimated cost of $200 million. The Australian Government's development policy, Australian aid promoting prosperity, reducing poverty, and enhancing stability, recognizes that tertiary education is a crucial component of any investment in development. Australia Awards Short Courses are targeted programs of intensive training for selected cohorts to address specific technical or soft skills gaps. They are formal study or training opportunities, generally of less than three months, delivered by an approved Australian higher education provider or an Australian Registered Training Organization in Australia and/or partner countries. Australia Awards Short Courses are managed and administered by DFAT's overseas posts.

The program combines the scholarships offered by the Department of Foreign Affairs (DFAT), the Department of Education, and the Australian Centre for International Agricultural Research (ACIAR). Another good option for studying in Australia is the Destination Australia Program (DAP.) This scholarship is a part of the Australian Government's program that funds qualified tertiary educational institutions to offer scholarships for domestic and international students to study in regional Australia. Destination Australia scholarships can reimburse up to $15,000 per student per year and are available for students enrolling in a wide range of degrees, like a Certificate IV or PhD. This funding lasts up to four years in regional campus locations across Australia. Furthermore, Provider scholarships are regularly offered by Australian education providers for eligible international students based on their academic merit. You can consult with the admissions department or international office at the provider you are applying to for detailed advice and information.

If you're not interested in Australia, New Zealand also offers amazing scholarship programs and grants for international students. The New Zealand Scholarships for the current academic term, 2023 to 2024, are open for applicants, and they have shared a list of 5,000 fully funded New Zealand Scholarships for 2023. The NZ Scholarships are open for international applicants. New Zealand Scholarships are now available for Bachelor, Master, PhD, and Post-Doctoral degree programs. Most of these scholarships are supported and financed by the Government of New Zealand.

Additionally, New Zealand has an outstanding education system and internationally recognized qualifications. This country has a lot to offer in terms of academic merit. You must apply online for the Fully Funded Scholarships in New Zealand. The best part about studying in New Zealand is that you are not expected to stay or return to the country for work after you get your degree.

International students can apply for the New Zealand Government Visa Sponsorship Jobs. The duration of the New Zealand Scholarship is four years, and abroad students get two years for a master's degree. All programs offered through this scholarship are in English, which is another reason to pursue your education in New Zealand. There are only eight universities in New Zealand, and they don't get many applicants, which gives you higher chances of acceptance and grants. The University of Auckland International Student Excellence Scholarships is a new program for international undergraduate and graduate students. The grant can go up to $10,000 towards compulsory tuition fees. The duration of the Scholarship is two years, and they plan to award up to 50 Scholarships annually.

The New Zealand Government Scholarships are offered for Undergraduate, Master, and doctoral degree programs. New

Zealand offers scholarships to eligible citizens from developing countries to study abroad at a New Zealand education institution or university or at a Pacific university. Additionally, the Scholarships for Undergraduate and Postgraduate study are full tertiary scholarships for eligible international students to study full-time at a New Zealand education institution or a Pacific university. The Short-Term Training Scholarships for Pacific and Timor-Leste citizens are short grants for training skills and on-the-job work experience for workers from eligible Pacific countries and Timor-Leste. Moreover, the Short-Term Training Scholarships for citizens of Southeast Asia and Timor-Leste are short scholarships for skills training for workers from eligible Southeast Asian countries and Timor-Leste.

Apart from these funding opportunities, the English Language Training for Officials Scholarships (NZELTO) is also a short scholarship for government officials from eligible African and Asian countries to come to New Zealand for English language training. The University of Otago Scholarships are available for international applicants, who can apply anytime to study in New Zealand without worrying about a deadline. Furthermore, Otago University offers 200 Doctoral scholarships for domestic and international students from all over the world. Candidates pursuing professional doctorates and PhDs are eligible to apply for scholarships at the University of Otago in 2023. The Wellington Scholarships in New Zealand cover any program offered by the university, including doctoral programs. This scholarship provides substantial financial support, making it an excellent opportunity for advancing academic pursuits.

In short, you don't have to be afraid of living your best life in the university of your dreams because you're short on funding. Several accredited universities offer affiliated financial aid options and scholarships that give eligible and qualified students opportunities. You must find the right program for you!

Chapter 4:

Study Abroad Checklist for the USA

The decision to pursue a degree in the United States is a defining moment in your personal, academic, and career goals.

The Institute of International Education (IIE) states that more than 1.1 million students are inclined toward earning an advanced degree in the United States. There are various reasons, including a spectrum of opportunities. However, weighing the pros and cons of moving to a new country can be intimidating.

Before considering moving to the USA to attend a college or university, thoroughly evaluate the advantages, challenges, and opportunities you might encounter to make an informed decision and take the next step toward a successful future.

Studying in the US would grant you access to advanced language skills and valuable intercultural experiences. It would open the doors to one of the best higher education systems in the world, with access to cutting-edge technology and research. This would, in turn, augment your comprehension, problem-solving skills, and knowledge of modern practices within your field.

Higher education in the United States is renowned for offering students a wide range of degree options. For this reason, students have every opportunity to choose a program of study that caters to their interests and goals that may not be available to them in other countries.

If you are from a developing country that has limited resources, studying in the United States will help you connect with all kinds of resources that will provide you with an opportunity to learn, grow, and gain access to tools that will set you apart from the students in the rest of the world.

Most American universities feature a plethora of elective and complementary programs, often in affiliation with other colleges and universities in their region or consortium. This way, you have the chance to explore coursework beyond your major.

Even if your goal is not to immigrate to the United States, having the experience of studying and working in the U.S. could potentially make you a more desirable job candidate when returning to your home country, especially if you work for a global company.

International students can take advantage of their experiential learning, co-operations, and internships to harness real-world experience in their field of choice.

This paves the way for valuable learning opportunities and can also build bridges with future employers who could potentially sponsor you for a work visa.

STEM-eligible degrees can allow international students to stay in the U.S. for an additional two years post-graduation, beyond the standard allowance of one year, while underemployment in a U.S.-based company.

F-1 students with eligible science, technology, engineering, and mathematics (STEM) degrees from Student and Exchange Visitor Program certified universities have the chance to apply for optional practical training (OPT). This STEM OPT extension allows these students to stay in the United States for an additional 24 months (totaling 36 months) to receive practical training. This is a paid internship and is related to their field of study.

If you're a non-native English speaker, you can fully immerse yourself in learning this new language. Perfecting your skills will help you gain a competitive advantage in the job market. Being multilingual makes you a valuable asset to any organization as it exhibits your cross-cultural communication skills.

Studying at an American university allows students to expand their global network, experience new cultures, and gain a global perspective.

The United States is a melting pot of different cultures, races, and ethnicities. This diverse environment eliminates all kinds of discrimination and opens the doors for acceptance into all communities. The U.S. is a huge country comprising diverse landscapes, cultures, and experiences. If you choose to study in the U.S., you will tap many opportunities to travel and explore the fascinating sights and sounds.

Considering all the factors mentioned earlier, the United States is an excellent option as a study destination. It will help you in your personal and professional growth.

Now,

Let's explore the top 5 university rankings in the United States. These schools offer you an excellent education at a great price and nurture students to become successful entrepreneurs and influential leaders in their respective fields.

1- Massachusetts Institute of Technology (MIT)

MIT is a leading university committed to educating students in science, technology, and related fields that serve the modern world. Many of the world's top minds include Nobel Prize-winning physicist

Richard Feynman, Prime Minister of Italy Mario Draghi, and world-renowned architect I. M. Pei attended MIT.

2- Stanford University

Located on the outskirts of Palo Alto, California, this world-class university is renowned for its STEM programs, which have produced several Nobel Prizes, Turing Awards, and Fields Medal recipients. Some of the graduates of Stanford include billionaire venture capitalist Peter Thiel, Instagram cofounder Kevin Systrom, U.S. senator Cory Booker, and the first female supreme court justice, Sandra Day O'Connor.

3- University of California, Berkeley

The University of California Berkeley is famous for leading technological and social change. The faculty at UC Berkeley was responsible for the discovery of Vitamins E and K, the development of the atomic bomb, and the creation of the flu vaccine. The university comprises over 150 departments and eight interdisciplinary research facilities across five colleges. Berkeley faculty boasts 4 Pulitzer Prize winners.

4- Princeton University

The fourth oldest college is a leading private research university. Princeton shows commitment to service through learning and professional and community connections. Princeton has produced 21 Rhodes scholars over the last ten years and has produced 18 total alumni Nobel Prize winners.

5- Columbia University

Upper Manhattan, Columbia's crown jewel, is an Ivy League University. This school's location helps provide students with a wealth of resources and learning opportunities. Columbia has produced more Nobel Laureates than any other university in the Ivy League. Columbia alums include five founding fathers, 34 presidents, prime ministers, and nine supreme court justices.

Let's go over the school entry requirements for U.S. universities.

You must meet the minimum academic and English language requirements to gain admission to a US degree program.

6- Harvard University

Harvard University is a private Ivy League research university in Cambridge, Massachusetts. It is the oldest institution of higher learning in the United States and one of the world's most prestigious and highly-ranked universities.

Academic Qualifications

You need to have good grades in your previous academic record, equivalent to the minimum Grade Point Average (GPA) for entry to your program of choice.

English Language Requirements

With advanced English language proficiency, you will have the necessary background to start a bachelor's or master's degree immediately. Generally, scores from any of the following English language exams are accepted:

1. TOEFL (Test of English as a Foreign Language)
2. Kaplan iBT
3. IELTS (International English Language Testing System)
4. IELTS Indicator
5. Pearson Test of English (PTE)
6. Duolingo English Test (DET)

Finding the right degree program is a career path that is essential to determine the outcomes of your academic and personal future.

A college major is a specific subject area that students specialize in. Typically, between one-third and one-half of the courses you'll take in college will be in your major related to it. You can choose one of the following majors:

Arts and Humanities

Programs in art and humanities take a multidisciplinary approach to education. They combine the study of languages, literature, art, music, philosophy, and religion.

Business

Business programs involve teaching students the skills and operations of the business industry. They include studies in various areas, including accountancy, finance, marketing, human resources, economics, etc.

Health and Medicine

Programs in health and medicine focus on the study, research, and knowledge of health principles and the application of corresponding expertise to prevent, diagnose, and care for humans and animals.

Multi-Interdisciplinary Studies

Programs in multi-disciplinary areas of study combine two or more programs through a common theme and allow students to specialize their degree to their interests.

Public and Social Services

Students learn to analyze, manage, and provide public programs and services in this study area. Areas of focus include law and legal studies, public administration, social services, protective services, and more.

Science, Technology, Engineering, and Math

Programs in STEM include majors in four disciplines: Science, technology, engineering, and math. The skills needed for each domain overlap, and studies in these fields provide students with a multidisciplinary skill set.

Social Sciences

This field of study is where students learn how to focus on how individuals behave within society, how society works, and the relationship between the two.

U.S Scholarships for International Students

Scholarships or funding opportunities can be invaluable for students aspiring to study in the United States.

The first step towards availing a funding opportunity is to contact your school's financial aid office. Various colleges offer scholarship programs specifically for international students attending their institutions.

The eligibility for a scholarship depends entirely on the scholarship itself. Some scholarships require students to possess a certain English and other test score, some have specific country requirements, and some ask for a certain Grade Point Average.

Most scholarship programs require you to complete an application form, others require a specific written piece of work, while some require you to pursue studies in a particular field.

Once you have secured admission to your university of choice, you will need to get all your documents in order.

These include your:

- Passport
- Curriculum Vitae/résumé
- Certificates of graduation
- Letters of recommendation
- Transcripts

- Scorecards for entrance exams
- Scores on your English Proficiency Test
- Work experience letters
- Statement of Purpose (SOP)
- Essays
- Evidence of funds
- Proposal for Research/Portfolio/Project Description
- Certificates for extracurricular activities
- Copy of the application of confirmation

Post-Graduate Visa Options for International Students

If you decide to stay and work in the United States after completing your degree. There are a few visa options available to you. Some of them are discussed below:

Practical Training on an F1 Visa

An F1 student is generally entitled to a year of post-graduation practical training. Authorization for this type of training may be granted for 12 months. The department that deals with international students at your university will inform you of all the different training options available. You can also apply for an extension if you are in a STEM field.

Non-Immigrant H-3 Visa (for trainees)

An H-3 visa is tailored for those individuals who do not have the relevant education or work experience. It is for students interested in coming to the U.S. to train in a particular field with the intention of transporting that knowledge back to their home country upon completing their visa.

Non- Immigrant H-1B Visa (Specialty occupation)

To obtain this type of visa, you need to be:

A U.S employer to sponsor the applicant

A U.S bachelor's degree holder or an equivalent

A correlation between the job duties and the applicant's education and work experience

The H-1B visa is granted for an initial period of 3 years and can be given an extension for another three years, but it cannot be extended for more than six years.

Employment-Based Immigration

To obtain an employment-based immigration visa, an applicant must apply for a specific labor certification. This is often a strenuous process and may take years, based on jurisdiction.

Advanced Degree Professions/ Exceptional Ability

Applicants with advanced degrees (Master's or Bachelor's, plus five years of work experience) can apply for this category.

An F1 visa holder can secure a PR/citizenship if they receive an employer sponsorship, marry a US citizen, seek asylum, win the green card lottery, receive sponsorship from a relative who owns a business, participate in military service, or receive a parent or child sponsorship.

Job Opportunities for Students in the United States

A vast majority of part-time opportunities are available for students who wish to find work along with their academia. The highest paying are working as a campus ambassador, barista, teaching assistant, library assistant, receptionist, research or study assistant, department assistant, catering assistant, sales assistant, or tutor/peer mentor.

The federal minimum wage is $7.25 per hour, but each state sets its wage laws. Therefore, where you choose to study will significantly impact your income.

There are some limitations when you work as an international student. Students with F-1 visas can generally work on campus at their university for a maximum of 20 hours a week during the term. During holidays, this can exceed up to 40 hours a week.

Becoming an international student in the US is not an easy job. The application process is lengthy, but with the proper guidance, you can achieve personal, academic, and career success that would define your future.

So, get ready to embark on your journey, apply to your university of choice, and go ahead and pack your bags for the opportunity of a lifetime!

The Journey To Becoming A Billionaire

Studies show that international or immigrant students initiated most of America's greatest startups. A few examples of such students and enterprises:

- Noubar Afeyan from MIT started Moderna Therapeutics.
- Ash Ashutosh Penn State started Actifio.
- Mohit Aron Rice started Nutanix.
- Alexander Asseily from Stanford started Jawbone.
- Amr Awadallah from Stanford started Cloudera.
- Nicolas Desmarais from Amherst started AppDirect.

There are some things, especially regarding funding, that you must know before you apply to the US.

Tuition Fee

This will be the primary expenditure a student must face and will probably be among the highest. However, the amount of tuition fee would largely depend on the course and the university, along with any scholarships granted to the applicant. America has a broad categorization into two when it comes to universities – public and private. A public university is cheaper than a private one but more challenging to enroll into. Anyone who's already gotten into a college would know the fee structure, and anyone planning to apply should investigate its tuition fee before concluding. An estimated figure revolved between USD 8,000 to USD 55,000 per annum. A comprehensive list of the annual tuition fees of each program is mentioned below in USD:

Undergraduate	(20,000—40,000)
Graduate	(20,000—45,000)
Doctoral	(28,000—55,000)

Community colleges cost around $6000 to $20,000 per year, while an English course will cost you $700 to $2,000 monthly.

Like most countries, generalized courses such as humanities and education courses are cheaper. On the other hand, specialized courses such as engineering and medicine are likely to be relatively more expensive, an MBA being this expensive. Similarly, post-graduate studies are much more costly than undergraduate courses on a per annum scale but shorter in duration. It is highly recommended to also apply for scholarships. You never know when you will get lucky!

Visa Costs

It is best to consult a counselor regarding the student visa process, as it must not be fiddled with. A valid student comes with its costs and can cost an application fee of USD 160.

Accommodation Costs

It is preferable that students, especially international ones, opt for on-campus accommodation facilities. It is much more affordable and would be much easier for you to connect with those around you and suit your educational requirements. Being around both international and native students from similar courses will enhance your social life, bring you easy help, and allow you to settle conveniently in a country you are clueless about – in short, it's a great way to make friends quickly!

The only challenge posed is that not everyone would get access to this facility, which is primarily decided based on score or on a first-come-first-serve basis. It is essential to book a slot for yourself as early as possible.

If a student desires to live off-campus, the most common options include renting an apartment with shared roommates (generally from the same university or ethnicity) or a homestay with a local family. Whether on-campus or off-campus, a university will usually assist its students in finding accommodation. As with anywhere else, accommodation costs will vary from region to region, but students can consider approximately US $6000 to $14,000 annually while preparing their budget.

Living Expenses

Living expenses cover a variety of sub-categories but essentially refer to all things you need to survive in a city, such as food, transportation, toiletries, social activities, etc. It is a good practice to set a budget beforehand and document each expense not to overspend.

Considering all costs, a student budget for one lies between US $10,000 to $20,000 each academic year. A comprehensive breakdown of the list of expenses per month is as follows:

Food and Drinks	($2500)
Clothing	($500)
Books and Stationery	($500 – $1,000)
Transport	($500 – $1200)
Other	($2,000)

Test Requirements

The SAT is a standardized test widely used for college admissions in the United States. The SAT is a globally recognized college admission test that shows colleges what you know and how well you can apply that knowledge. A student taking the SAT can expect a reading, writing, and math comprehension test.

An alternative to the SAT is the GRE. The Graduate Record Examinations is a standardized test that is an admissions requirement for many graduate schools in the United States, Canada, and a few other countries. It measures your verbal reasoning, quantitative reasoning, critical thinking, and analytical writing skills.

Sports Scholarships

University sport in America is at the highest in the world level, so the universities carefully select promising candidates for their sports teams and, even more carefully, those whose education and training they will Fund.

Athletes who are trained in the US universities will receive the following:

- Condensed for time, but a complete knowledge, a training program.
- A minimum of 20 hours of training per week.
- Individual study schedules are based on the plan of training and competitions.
- Training with the best coaches and regular participation in competitions.
- To qualify for a sports scholarship, you must:
- Have outstanding sports results.
- Know English at the level corresponding to the admission requirements of the University.

- Pass the tests SAT/ACT/GRE subject tests at the level of entrance requirements.
- Have the grades, i.e., GPA, at the level of entrance requirements.
- Demonstrate discipline, high motivation, and excellent knowledge of the sport.

Even though funding is essential, you might be tempted to apply to the US after learning some fun facts about the country. For example:

1. The US flag was designed by a 17-year-old boy, Robert G. Heft.
2. Do you know that the US serves 100 acres of pizza every day?
3. The Harvard Library is the most extensive academic library in the world.
4. The US has the maximum number of entrepreneurs in the world.
5. One hundred eighty-two places in the US have ‘Christmas’ in their name.
6. While the official state animal of California is a grizzly bear, there have been no grizzly bears since 1922.
7. Someone has control of your GPS – who? The US.
8. Wish to try authentic Chinese food? Go to Manhattan’s Chinatown – it has the most Chinese residents in the Western Hemisphere.
9. The US is where you’ll find the most obese people.
10. Philadelphia was the original capital of the US.

Chapter 5:

Study Abroad Checklist for Canada

Canada is one of the best places you could pick for studying abroad. You would want to go to Canada for many reasons.

Enjoy the best quality of life

Canada has the highest standard of living in the world. International students enjoy the same privileges, rights, and freedom that benefit Canadian citizens. This country respects human rights, diversity, equality, stability, and peace!

According to the U.S. News & World Report in 2022, Canada ranks third on a global scale for the best quality of life (U.S. News & World Report, 2022).

Home to flexible and high-quality educational opportunities

Canada is famous for providing high-quality education and research opportunities between elementary and post-secondary studies. You can also enjoy the flexibility to transfer between different types and levels of education without facing certain hurdles common in other parts of the world. Additionally, you can choose from over 8,000 colleges and 16,000 university programs. About seven Canadian universities are ranked among the top 200 universities in the world.

A welcoming, diverse, and inclusive environment

Canada is known for being an open, safe, and culturally diverse space. You'll feel at home in the communities and classrooms. The country is home to more than 250 ethnic origins with 200 languages from all over the world. Almost 70 indigenous languages are spoken in Canada.

Choose from a series of affordable options

Canada offers a series of affordable and accessible scholarships and work opportunities to help international students pay for their education. Many programs also offer work placements or internships for students to get hands-on experience as they study. Most international students are eligible to work while they study. They can get a Post-Graduation Work Permit after their studies. Moreover, the tuition fees are generally lower than in colleges and universities in Australia, the U.K., and the U.S.

Apart from the environment and affordable education, Canada is home to some of the top universities in the world!

1. University of Toronto

The top university in Canada is the University of Toronto, ranking 25th worldwide. The university climbed four places in this year's rankings and earns high scores across most indicators, especially academic reputation, where it ranks 15th worldwide.

2. McGill University

McGill University is in Montreal and remains in second place in Canada this year. It rose four spots in the rankings to 31st place. McGill University produced 12 Nobel laureates and 145 Rhodes Scholars among its alums and Canada's current prime minister, Justin Trudeau.

3. University of British Columbia

One of the top three universities in the country is the University of British Columbia, which ranks third in Canada and 45th in the whole world. It rose six places this year. Now, it ranks 28th in the world for the academic reputation indicator. The University of British Columbia embraces innovation and challenges the status quo.

4. Université de Montréal

Université de Montréal ranks fourth among Canada's top universities. It is a French-language public research university in Montreal, founded in 1878, and it has over 67,350 students, including 10,000 international students.

5. University of Alberta

The University of Alberta holds the 119th spot. It welcomes 40,000 students across its four campuses. Its highest score comes from the international faculty indicator.

After you decide which university you wish to go to, you need to check the eligibility criteria and the requirements that you must meet to get in. You can check to see if the university of your choice is a Designated Learning Institution (DLI). This will show you whether Canada recognizes the university as a credible institution and won't indulge international students in educational scams.

Another thing you need to look out for is the tuition fee. Tuition fees can add a lot to your costs of studying. They vary depending on the country you're applying to, but universities offer more details about their tuition on their websites for each of their academic programs. Additionally, it's better to research the subject you want to study and the language of study. Canada is a bilingual state, so that you can pick a Master's degree in English, French, or both.

Moreover, high grades are essential for your application process. Many Canadian institutions require 70% or above the average score. The higher your percentage, the higher your chances of enrollment in a prestigious university. If you are over 25 and have graduated from your last program at least two years before your application process, you will be asked to provide information about your previous employment.

Since students in Canada can choose from a wide range of English as well as French-taught Master's degrees, they have to prove their proficiency level through different language tests. The main English language tests accepted by top universities in Canada include:

- IELTS Academic
- PTE Academic
- C1 Advanced
- TOEFL iBT
- Some universities also accept other English tests, like:
- CAEL (Canadian Academic English Language Assessment)
- CanTEST (Canadian Test of English for Scholars and Trainees)
- MELAB (Michigan English Language Assessment Battery)
- French tests accepted by universities in Canada
- DALF
- DELF
- TEF
- TCF

You must also be careful while picking the study program of your choice. This can be tricky because Canadian universities offer many different types of programs with unique features. However, there are certain things to look out for during this process.

Do you know what you want to be when you grow up?

This is a difficult question because most people still don't know what they want in their life or careers. But finding out your career path can be fun because this means you can try different subjects and courses that can lead you in a direction you never thought was possible. So, if you're unsure about what you wish to study, choose a program that offers flexibility in selecting courses.

Are scholarships available?

This is perhaps one of the most important factors when choosing a study program. There are many opportunities for scholarships in Canada for international students. If this is a priority, make sure to check out what your prospective department or program is offering.

How does a Canadian study program help your overall career goals?

When you have a clear idea of your future career goals, you can focus on programs that can assist you in getting there. You can look through university and college course listings and read their detailed descriptions to understand what's covered in a program.

Where do you wish to study?

If you feel like there are too many good programs to choose from, try planning based on where you want to live and look at the study options in that area.

Is this program compatible with your life right now?

Most international students in Canada bring their families along with them, or they have work commitments during their studying years. Finding a study program that fits your current lifestyle is the key to finding the perfect program that caters to your needs.

Once you pick the perfect program, you need to start looking for scholarship options. Luckily, Canada offers a multitude of financial aid and scholarship programs!

1. Banting Postdoctoral Fellowships

- Given to national and international post-graduates to attract top-tier intelligent minds.
- Students are given 70,000 CAD annually for two years.

2. IDRC Research Awards

- Students from developing countries can apply for this scholarship.
- A sum amount is transferred throughout your course tenure.

3. Vanier Canada Graduate Scholarships Program

- The government of Canada offers scholarships to students pursuing Masters in the fields of Science, Engineering, Humanities, etc.
- The scholarship presents 50,000 CAD annually to students for three years.

4. Shastri Indo-Canadian Institute

- Fellowships to various graduate and postgraduate Indian students studying at a reputed university.
- Eligible students can sign up for courses or participate in online coaching from any Canadian university under SICI.

5. Canadian Commonwealth Scholarship and Fellowship Plan

- Students hailing from the commonwealth nations can avail of several grants every year.
- This scholarship changes every year to provide different privileges.

6. Ontario Graduate Scholarship Program

- The Ontario scholarship provides grants to students who enroll in Ontario public universities.
- You can get from 5000 CAD - 15 000 CAD.

7. Ontario Trillium Scholarship

- International PhD students are awarded this scholarship.
- Up to 40,000 CAD is given across four years.

8. Canada-ASEAN SEED

- Global Affairs Canada gives out scholarships to students pursuing their higher studies.
- Cost of Visa and/or study/work permit fees, airfare, health insurance, living expenses, ground transportation expenses, books, and supplies are included.

9. Quebec Provincial Government Scholarship

- Financial assistance to students studying in Quebec is covered. (The scholarship has currently been paused.)
- Scholarships of up to 40,000 CAD are granted.
- National Research Council of Canada (NRCC)
- Research grants are given to research students pursuing their master's or PhD's.
- The price and duration depend on your study level.

The best part about studying in Canada is that you don't only enjoy the accessible and affordable higher education opportunities but also enjoy post-graduate job opportunities in the country! To work in Canada after you graduate, you need a work permit. The work experience you gain while working may help you qualify for permanent residence.

Post-graduation work permit (PGWP)

Graduates of certain designated learning institutions are eligible for this work permit.

Canadian Experience Class

This is operated through the Express Entry immigration system. The Canadian Experience Class (CEC) program is one of the quickest ways to obtain Canadian permanent residence. There is a range of eligibility factors that you must qualify for to apply for this program, including age, language proficiency, and level of education. A distinctive requirement is that applicants prove they have at least 12 months of continuous, full-time, and skilled work experience in Canada within the previous three years or an equivalent amount of part-time experience. Once an international student obtains this level of work experience, CEC may become an ideal immigration option.

Federal Skilled Worker Program

This is operated through the Express Entry immigration system. The Federal Skilled Worker (FSW) program can be an option for international student graduates. Unlike the Canadian Experience Class (CEC), FSW does not need a person to have Canadian work experience, so this is a good option for international student graduates who already gained skilled work experience abroad. The FSW program is based on merit, and it is an immigration program that uses a points-based Comprehensive Ranking System (CRS) score to rank applicants against one another, only accepting candidates with the most competitive applications to apply for permanent residence. If an international student meets the eligibility requirements and is within the CRS scoring system, FSW can be an accessible pathway to becoming a permanent resident.

It is important to note that the FSW program requires applicants to prove that they have a minimum of 12 months of full-time, continuous, and skilled work experience, not limited to Canada or an equivalent amount of part-time experience. However, this program is not an option for international students who have never entered the workforce.

Provincial Nominee Programs

Each of Canada's provinces and territories has its own unique immigration programs. These are called Provincial Nominee Programs (PNPs). Every PNP has a different way of working and structuring to meet the needs of that specific province or territory. Many PNPs offer preference to applicants with a link to the province, including previous study programs completed within the region and work experience gained there. International students may be eligible to apply for a PNP within a province, depending on the area where they completed their study program.

Prominent courses to explore

- I.T./Computer Engineering
- VFX & Multimedia
- Mechanical Engineering
- Renewable Energy
- Project Management
- Food Science
- Nursing and Pharmacy
- Supply Chain Management
- Financial Planning

Important facts to know before you apply

- Months for academic Intakes fall in the fall (September), winter (January), and summer (May.)
- There are a total of 223 universities in Canada, and collectively, they house more than 750,000 international students.
- The average tuition fee is CAD 18,000 per annum, and the average cost of living is CAD 10,000 per annum.

Student Life

If you choose a Canadian university for higher education, you can experience life to the fullest in a country home to 750,000+ international students. Imagine the cultural diversity and richness.

As a student in Canada, you can never be out of the league to enjoy life to its fullest. Be it attending lectures laden with team tasks or hanging out in the cafeteria or study lounges or the sports arena on the campus of your college or university; you are bound to make new friends, learn about new cultures, languages and, certainly enjoy a few games of ice hockey and baseball, during the season.

Be it restaurants or theatres in the downtowns of Toronto, Montreal, Vancouver, Ottawa, or Calgary, or be it a round of ice skating on the Rideau Canal in Ottawa or be it trekking around the gorges around the Banff National Park, you will never feel out of sorts, once you are in Canada. From preparing your meals to shopping for your daily groceries to hustling between studies, work, and home, the 'student life' in Canada will transform you into everything you and your family would take pride in. Yes, once in Canada, do not forget to register with the Embassy or the Consulate Offices.

Visa Process

1. Study Permit

This is for students who want to study in Canada for over six months. You should apply for a study permit when you receive your acceptance letter from a designated learning institution. In this way, you can arrive in Canada up to four weeks before the start of your program.

2. Student Partnership Program (SPP) visa

This is for students from designated countries who want to study in Canada for more than six months. The best time to apply for the Student Direct Stream (SDS) visa is when you have been accepted into a participating Canadian educational institution. You can arrive in Canada up to four weeks before the start of your program.

Canada is one of the world's best countries for higher education, especially for students from third-world countries. For almost one and a half decades, Canada has undeniably emerged as the most sought-after study destination for students from more than 100 countries.

Indian students currently account for 34% of the total international students in Canada, and the number is only growing at 21% per year. Since 2017, Indian nationals have been at the top of the chart regarding obtaining Canadian Permanent Residence.

Canada is known for its state-of-the-art education infrastructure, which, coupled with the best instructors, leads to the most desired academic output for international students and their families. With an array of credentials, ranging from Diplomas, Advanced Diploma, Associate Degrees, Bachelor's, Post Graduate Diploma, and Master's, there is no dearth in the quality and diversity of excellent program choices for students at Canada's Universities and its Community (Government) Colleges.

If you are leaning towards Canada for your higher studies, then you have the best resources and open-minded programs at your disposal!

Go through the list of best universities located in the country and pick the one that best suits your available funding, grades, lifestyle, and career choice. Be sure to check through and apply for the finest scholarship programs offered by your university of choice, and don't be afraid to have fun with your courses. The critical thing to remember is that you can permanently settle in one of the world's leading countries, which is beautiful and truest champions of human rights campaigns worldwide.

Chapter 6:

Study Abroad Checklist for the UK

Students worldwide get tempted to study in the UK, and there are multiple reasons for that! The UK is known for its high-quality education, diversity, and radiant student cities, making it a wonderful place to study abroad.

Recently, the UK has announced more incentives to attract international students, like visa changes and lenient immigration policies. The country hopes to recruit 600,000 international students per year by 2030. Between 2019 and 2020, international university students comprised about 22% of the student population. Universities in the UK are known for their medicine, arts, and humanities courses, and there are more than 100 universities for international students to choose from.

The UK is incredibly diverse. Fourteen percent of the population in the UK was born abroad, which adds up to about 9.5 million people. This shows that international students who move overseas to the UK can learn about various cultures and make friends with people around the world.

The most prominent advantage of studying in the UK is that there are many career opportunities, especially if you work on the UK's Shortage Occupation List. There is a shortage of nurses, pharmacists, teachers, and engineers in the UK, and the government actively recruits professionals for these positions from abroad.

The list of the world's top universities that reside in the UK is almost endless, but the following ones are the most known and sought after:

University of Oxford

Retaking first place in the UK this year is the University of Oxford, which drops one place in the global rankings to fifth. Achieving high scores across all indicators, Oxford is the highest-ranked school in the UK for faculty-student ratio (eighth place) and citations per faculty (44th place).

University of Cambridge

Cambridge is in second place, ranked seventh globally. However, Cambridge is the highest-ranked university in the UK for academic and employer reputation, in second place globally for these indicators.

Imperial College London

Taking the bronze medal position in the UK is Imperial College London, the highest-ranked university in the capital. It moves up one position globally this year to eighth place and ranks ninth for academic reputation.

UCL (University College London)

UCL ranks 10th globally, and its highest score can be found in the academic reputation indicator, where it places 13th in the world.

University of Edinburgh

Ranking fifth in the UK and remaining the 20th best university in the world is the University of Edinburgh – the only Scottish institution in the UK top 10. It scores particularly highly for academic and employer reputations, ranking 25th and 31st in the world, respectively, for these indicators.

The University of Manchester

The University of Manchester ranks sixth in the UK this year, taking joint 27th place in the global rankings. Employers look at Manchester graduates particularly favorably – the university ranks 21st in the world for the employer reputation indicator.

King's College London (KCL)

Seventh in the UK again this year is King's College London (KCL), which climbed two places in the global rankings to joint 31st. One of four London-based universities in the UK's top 10, KCL achieves impressive scores in all indicators, particularly academic reputation, where it ranks among the top 50 universities worldwide.

Choosing the right university is the first step towards choosing your career. But it can be an intimidating and confusing decision. The way to go about this is by breaking it down regarding location, rankings, and courses.

You must review the location of the university campus and housing while deciding on the university. Do you want to live in the central or suburban area? Are you considering moving to London, Wales, Glasgow, Cambridge, or Oxford? List down the pros and cons of each place you have short-listed, and pick a university that caters to your accommodation, transport, financial, and social needs.

It is common for students to choose a university according to its high ranking. Good ranking reflects certain levels of student satisfaction and teaching quality. For many international students, the university's reputation affects their chances of getting a good job in their home country. You can even communicate with your friends who studied at one of the universities to see if the university's reputation corresponds with their experience. Even a top-ranking university may not have the best to offer in your chosen program.

Lastly, it is vital that you overview the modules that you want to study. Many universities offer the same courses, but they can hold different types of content based on the university that gives them. Other professors may teach modules and may be tested in different ways. Some universities offer placement opportunities, and some do not provide specific modules.

Breaking down your decision process based on these values can help you make a sound and informed decision without being overwhelmed.

Once you decide which of these top universities you see yourself attending, you must become well-versed in the requirements for studying at these universities.

English Proficiency Tests are the most important and standard requirements for studying in the UK. All universities and courses require international students to produce proof of English proficiency by submitting scores of exams like the International English Language Testing System (IELTS), the Test of English as a Foreign Language (TOEFL), and the Pearson Test of English Academic (PTE Academic). While these are some commonly accepted English tests for admissions, students can submit Duolingo English Tests, Cambridge Certificate of Proficiency in English (CPE), and Trinity Secure English Language Tests (SELTs).

Students who want to pursue higher education in the UK after finishing high school must complete their 10+2 education from a recognized school and possess the minimum marks and eligibility requirements to study in their chosen program and university.

Requirements to study in the UK at the undergraduate level:

- Certificate for completing 10+2 education from a recognized Indian board with minimum marks.
- Original academic transcripts from previous academic institutions.

- Statement of Purpose
- Letters of Recommendations
- Scores of English Proficiency Tests
- Passport and other ID proof
- Bank statements to provide evidence of Financial Funds
- Offer Letter
- Student visa

Apart from requirements, you must know how to fund your education in the UK. Tuition fees can be too much for one to bear, which is why the UK offers a myriad of feasible scholarship programs that can help international students achieve their dreams abroad.

Chevening Scholarships

Chevening Scholarships, the UK government's global scholarship program, are awarded to outstanding scholars from Chevening-eligible countries worldwide. Awards are typically for a one-year Master's degree. Most Chevening Scholarships cover tuition fees, a living allowance at a set rate (for one individual), an economy class return airfare to the UK, and additional grants to cover essential expenditures.

Scotland Saltire Scholarships

The Scottish Government, in collaboration with Scottish universities, is offering Scotland's Saltire Scholarships to citizens from Canada, China (including Hong Kong), India, Japan, Pakistan, and USA who wish to study full-time Masters degrees fully delivered in Scottish universities, in the areas of science, technology, creative industries, healthcare and medical sciences, and renewable and clean energy. Each award is worth £8000 to be used towards tuition fees for the duration of 1 year of full-time study.

Commonwealth Masters Scholarships

The Commonwealth Scholarships are intended for students from developing Commonwealth countries who want to pursue Master's studies in the UK. These scholarships are funded by the UK Department for International Development (DFID). Each Scholarship provides airfare to and from the United Kingdom, tuition and examination fees, personal maintaining allowance, thesis grant (if applicable), and initial arrival allowance, among others.

GREAT scholarships

A GREAT scholarship is an award of £10,000 toward your tuition fee for a one-year Master's program in the UK. This scholarship is offered through a partnership between the British Government and participating universities. To apply, first, you should check if your country is one of the 14 eligible for this award. Then, access your university funding page and see if they offer the prize. If they do, follow the instructions there.

Simmons University Kotzen Scholarships

Simmons University Kotzen Scholarships is a fully funded scholarship for international students. This scholarship is offered for undergraduate studies. The scholarship covers full tuition, mandatory fees, and room and board.

Imperial College London PhD Scholarship

Imperial College London Ph.D. Scholarship is a fully funded scholarship institute for international students. Up to 10 fully-funded scholarships are awarded each year. This scholarship covers tuition fees and an annual tax-free contribution to maintenance costs of £16,553.

Once you understand which scholarship program best suits you, you have to get your visa requirements under control. The best way to not get confused is to have a detailed checklist.

You need to have a current passport or other valid travel documentation. Another thing to keep in mind is that you need to disclose the qualifications stated on your CAS. You should note that if no qualifications are listed in your CAS, you are not required to provide any.

You also need to give proof of your knowledge of the English language. Universities can choose how they assess a student's knowledge of English. Your CAS will confirm how the university has assessed your English language ability. If it has been evaluated by you providing a certificate or qualification, then this will be listed in your CAS, and you must provide the certificate listed. If no English language qualifications are listed in your CAS, you will not need to provide any with your application.

Another thing that you can't overlook is translations. If any document is not in English, the original must be accompanied by a complete translation. The translation must contain:

- Validation from the translator that it is an exact translation of the original document
- Translation company's contact details
- The date of the translation

Then, you need to provide proof of finances. You need to prove that you have a specific amount of money available for tuition fees and living costs in the UK. See our information on the financial requirements for guidance on how to check what this amount is.

The types of documents that you can submit to prove your finances are:

- Personal bank statements or building society statements
- Bank letters
- Official loan letters
- Official financial sponsorship letters

You also have to provide a letter of consent from your government sponsor. If you have received any official financial sponsorship from a government in the past year, you must provide a letter from this sponsor confirming the sponsor's consent to make the Student Visa application.

You must also submit an ATAS (Academic Technology Approval Scheme certificate). This is a certificate required by some postgraduate students. You should note that an ATAS certificate takes approximately one month to be issued. Your CAS will confirm if you need an ATAS certificate.

This checklist may seem like a lot, but the benefits of graduating in the UK outweigh all the items on the list, especially the UK's diverse work visas offered to international students. Five types of work visa options may be available to you if you study in the UK.

Tier 2 (General) visa is the most common work visa for international students to remain and work in the UK after their studies. This visa aims to fill the shortage in the UK labor market. Therefore, applicants must meet a minimum salary of £21,000+ per year, and their employer must be a licensed Tier 2 sponsor to sponsor their work visa.

Tier 4 Doctorate Extension Scheme allows PhD students who complete their studies to stay in the UK for a further 12 months. Graduates can use this time to look for jobs, work to gain practical work experience, or set up a business as an entrepreneur.

Tier 5 (Youth Mobility Scheme) visa is designed to help young adults from certain countries experience life in the United Kingdom. This visa allows students from Australia, Canada, Hong Kong, Japan, Monaco, New Zealand, the Republic of Korea, or Taiwan to work in the UK for up to two years after graduation. There are limited places for this visa, and you cannot apply from inside the UK.

Start-up visa (replaces the formal Tier 1 (Graduate Entrepreneur) visa) is an option for international graduates who wish to develop ideas or entrepreneurial skills by setting up an innovative, viable, and scalable business in the UK. You must have an endorsement letter from your UK universities or a business organization with a history of supporting UK entrepreneurs.

Getting a work permit is simply the first step, and once you cross that bridge, you will be greeted with a wide array of lucrative job opportunities that can make your future!

Just as you need a Tier 4 student visa to study in the UK, you will have to apply for a Tier 2 (general) work visa to stay in the UK and get an eligible job with an approved employer. If you want to set up a business in the UK, you must apply for a Tier 1 visa. You have five years until your work permit expires, which you can use to build your future and plan to settle permanently in the UK.

The job market in the UK looks for fresh international graduates who can put their skills to use. The best industries that offer jobs for international students include:

Engineering

The UK provides state-of-the-art facilities to students to pursue education in Engineering. As one of the top destinations in the world to study Engineering, you will have the opportunity to conduct extensive research and learn with the help of practical training that prepares you for the job market.

Healthcare

The UK is known for its top-notch healthcare system. Healthcare professionals are in demand across the UK, and you can expect to receive rewarding service salaries. The responsibility attached to this profession and the intensity of the programs in this field are high and require great dedication.

Accountancy and Finance

Whether small or big, every company requires professionals to look after its finances. Therefore, Accounting and finance are among the most sought-after professions, with abundant job opportunities for international students in the UK.

Marketing and Sales

Competition for jobs in the field of marketing and sales is relatively high. There is wide scope in this field, and you can expect financial rewards, job satisfaction, and an opportunity to grow.

Overall, the UK is one of the top destinations for any international student. Once they pass the visa process, they can use the scholarship opportunities offered by the UK to live out their dreams in this diverse and colorful country!

Chapter 7:

Study Abroad Checklist for Australia

Whether it is an MBA, engineering degree, humanities, or English language course, Australia is among the best countries for higher education. One of the main reasons for this is that Australia is difficult to beat in terms of its standard of living, academic excellence, and support for international students.

The quality of life in Australia ranks secondary to only Norway as the best in the world. The country offers sophisticated infrastructure, state-of-the-art healthcare services, a varying range of public transport, numerous student services, and a relatively affordable cost of living. Australia is a hub for those looking to study abroad. The country promotes five of the world's 30 best cities for students regarding quality of life, employment opportunities, cost of living, and student community.

The Australian Government also offers various incentives for international students, including about $200 million worth of scholarships, job visas in diverse sectors, research opportunities, and achieving a permanent residency status after graduation. Australia has a national regulatory and quality agency for higher education known as the Tertiary Education Quality and Standards Agency (TEQSA). The Australian Government created it to surveil quality and monitor all forms of higher education providers through a series of standards and benchmarks set by the independent Higher Education Standards Panel. The Education Services for Overseas Students (ESOS) law upholds the following regulations:

- Well-being of all international students.
- Quality of students' academic experiences.
- Provision of accurate information.

When it comes to Australia, there is no lack of options regarding well-known and internationally recognized universities. Australia has 36 universities in the recently released QS World University Rankings 2021. Only six of the universities on this list have fallen in rank this year, with the majority of Australian universities showing noteworthy improvements. Some of the best universities in Australia include:

Australian National University (ANU)

Australian National University (ANU) is the top Australian university, scoring well across almost all indicators, including academic reputation, international faculty, international students, and citations per faculty ratio indicators, ranking within the top 50 worldwide.

University of Sydney

The University of Sydney is Australia's second-best university, and it rose two places this year, ranking 40th worldwide. It has perfect scores in the international faculty and international students' indicators. The University of Sydney was Australia's first university and is a member of the Group of Eight. It was established in 1850.

University of Melbourne

The University of Melbourne stands proud as the 41st top university in the world. It shines as the top-ranked university in Australia, earning high praise from academics and employers. Globally, it holds a strong position, landing 30th place out of 283 universities and making it into the top 30 list for its notable reputation. The university also ranks well in the international students' indicatór, and international students make up 42% of its student population, arriving from more than 130 countries.

University of New South Wales (UNSW)

In 44th place is the University of New South Wales (UNSW). It remains in fourth place in Australia. UNSW is a founding member of the Group of Eight, a group of Australian research-based universities. The university places in the top 50 for all but one of the indicators.

University of Queensland (UQ)

The university's alums include two Nobel laureates, Peter C. Dogerty and John Harsanyi; Academy Award winner Geoffrey Rush; and leaders in government, law, science, public service, and the arts. Researchers from UQ have been responsible for several recent innovations, such as the cervical cancer vaccine.

Monash University

It ranks among the world's 50 best universities for its academic reputation indicator and holds a perfect score in the international students' indicator. Monash University is located in Melbourne and has five campuses in the state of Victoria and two overseas, in Malaysia and South Africa.

University of Western Australia (UWA)

UWA beats all Australian universities above it for the proportion of international faculty members and the number of citations per faculty member, which measures research output).

University of Adelaide

The University of Adelaide was established in 1874, and it is Australia's third oldest university, placing 106th place in this year in the world university rankings. The University of Adelaide ranks 44th worldwide for the international students indicator, and more than 7,860 of the university's 21,142 students are international students from over 100 different countries.

University of Technology Sydney (UTS)

UTS scores exceptionally well in the citations per faculty, international students, and employer reputation indicators, ranking 67th, 78th, and 85th, respectively. UTS is one of the youngest top Australian universities. They aim to advance knowledge through research-inspired teaching, using their partnerships with industry, professions, and the community.

University of Wollongong

This university performs well for the citations per faculty indicator, ranking 75th globally. The University of Wollongong was founded initially in 1975 on the donations of local people. The university has partnered with its communities to make an impact in the Illawarra region and address society's economic, environmental, social, and medical challenges.

Entry Requirements:

Undergraduate Program

The candidate should have finished 12 years of schooling, matching the level of Australian qualification standards. They need to score at least 60% in four subjects to pass. They must get their degree from a recognized school.

Postgraduate (Masters) program:

Bachelor's degree attained from a recognized institute. The Bachelor's degree must be equivalent to an Australian Bachelor's

Degree deemed by qualification assessment references of your selected University. Minimum grades acquired in subjects required knowledge and working experience depending on the study program you have selected for admission.

Postgraduate (PhD) program:

Master's degree or Bachelor's honors degree must be equivalent to Australian qualification assessment references of your selected Australian University. The program you choose will determine the grades you need, the skills you must have, any research work required, the work experience you should possess, and the academic ability you need to show.

Language Requirements:

Australia is an English-speaking country; therefore, you will mostly find English-taught programs to study there at all academic levels. In countries where English is not a native language, students need to fulfill English proficiency requirements by passing one of the English language proficiency tests. IELTS course is accepted for admissions and student visas in Australia. Apart from IELTS, students can also do the following English language proficiency tests for admission to Australian Universities:

- Cambridge Advanced English (CAE),
- Pearson Test of English (PTE) Academic module,
- TOEFL Internet based Test (iBT)

The minimum grades and scores can be ascertained by Australian Universities for admission requirements. The minimum passing score for IELTS must be 6.0, with a writing grade of 5.5. Australian universities will only accept band scores of 5.0 or higher.

Documents Required for Admissions:

Australian universities accept admission applications directly submitted at their official website. The student must present an online application form and a PDF file of the required documents. The submission requirement may vary from one Australian university to another and according to the study program:

- Paid admission fee receipt
- Filled application form
- English language proficiency test certificate
- Copy of passport and national identity card
- Statement of intent, explaining why the applicant has chosen a specific study program for admissions
- Bank statement to prove that the person can afford tuition fees and living expenses
- Work experience, particularly in post-graduate courses
- Recommendation letters, which are written by the applicant's teacher stating the applicant's academic eligibility

Choosing the right program:

It always comes down to what you want to do in the future. It's vital to choose a field of study that aligns with the studies you have done previously and your career plans. Your choice should help you personally and professionally. Always keep in mind the employability prospects once the course is over. Your future plans about staying in Australia or returning home after your studies also influence your program of choice.

You can list the courses that suit you the most and start researching each course and the institutions that offer it. Almost every course and course details are listed on the college websites. Look through the information you have gathered and then choose the best option. The best option varies for every individual.

The duration of your course will have a direct impact on your stay in the country. Shorter duration programs will have shorter or no stay-back options. Longer programs will have more extended stay-back options. It will also decide the validity of your study permit or student visa in Australia and whether you need an extension.

The cost of tuition is a key thing to think about when choosing a program. Make sure to find out if the price you see is for one semester, one year, or the entire program. Knowing this will help you plan your budget right.

It would be best to research what city you want to go to. More developed territories mean more job opportunities and well-maintained public transportation but higher accommodation costs. Likewise, choosing an urban metropolitan city or a calm suburban vicinity will make all the difference during your stay in Australia.

A significant problem while planning a study trip abroad is funding. Australia offers multiple scholarships for international students that cover a range of expenses, starting from tuition fees and ending at accommodation.

Australia Awards:

The Australia Awards aim to promote knowledge, education links, and enduring ties between Australia and our neighbors through Australia's extensive scholarship programs. The program brings together scholarships offered by the Department of Foreign Affairs (DFAT), the Department of Education, and the Australian Centre for International Agricultural Research (ACIAR).

Destination Australia:

The Destination Australia Program (DAP) is an Australian Government program that funds eligible tertiary education providers to offer scholarships to domestic and international students to study in regional Australia. Destination Australia scholarships are valued at up to $15,000 per student per year and are available to students undertaking studies ranging from a Certificate IV to a Ph.D. for up to four years in regional campus locations across Australia.

Australian Government Research Training Program (RTP):

Learn more about the Research Training Program at the Department of Education website. Applications for these scholarships are made directly to a participating university.

Provider scholarships:

Australian education providers regularly offer scholarships to qualifying international students based on academic merit. Consult with the admissions team or international office at the provider you are applying to for further advice and information.

Application Process:

These high-ranking universities have a standardized process for each potential student. An application can be difficult and time-consuming, but having a checklist makes it easy to follow through. Here are some things to look out for:

- Completed Application Form.
- TOEFL/IELTS/PTE Exam Score.
- Academic Certificates (SSC, Inter, Bachelors)
- Photo Copies of the first and last pages of your passport.
- Job Experience Certificates (If available).
- Medium of Instruction (MOI).
- Any Other Documents.
- Application Form

For admission to Australian universities, you need to take the English language tests to prove your efficiency in English. With these Test Scores, the Universities assess the candidate's ability and skills to complete the course successfully. For any course like a master's or business program, you can take some popular English Language Tests like TOEFL, IELTS, or PTE.

You need to send the academic certificates in support of your educational qualifications. If you have just completed your higher secondary studies and are applying for undergraduate studies, you must send the SSC and higher secondary certificate to the university. And, if you have completed a bachelor's or Master's Degree, you need to send your degree certificate and the mark sheets. The Academic Certificates include the following:

- 10th Grade Transcripts & Certificate.
- 12th Grade Transcripts & Certificate.
- Bachelor's Transcripts & Degree (for Masters/PG Programs Only).
- Master's Transcripts and degree (if available).
- Diploma Transcripts and certificates (if available).
- Other Diplomas/Certificates (if available).
- Experience Certificates

If you are applying for any Business Program, you must have experience in the relevant field to get admission to any Business School in Australia. If you are applying for any undergraduate course, you don't need any experience. This Experience Certificate also helps in getting admission to any graduation program at Australian universities. It will push your application a little bit forward. The major documents in proof of work experience include:

- Latest Joining Letter.
- Latest Salary Slip.
- Employment Certificates from all Previous Employers.
- Experience letter.

Postgraduate Visa/Citizenship:

Many international students studying in Australia and staying in the country hope they will one day become permanent residents. However, students should remember that General Skilled Migration rules keep changing. This is an uncertain path, and there is no guarantee of getting Permanent residency after studying in Australia. The most common step for students is to get a post-study work visa after completing their studies. Then, they can apply for General Skilled Migration to achieve Permanent Residency (PR). There is too much information on General Skilled Migration/ Immigration/ Permanent Residency (PR) online. Sometimes, it's challenging to figure out your chances of gaining a Permanent Residency (PR.) It can be a long and tedious process, but it's not impossible. Also, the process proves to be very fruitful because Australia offers many high-paying job opportunities in diverse fields, especially for postgrad international students.

Job Opportunities:

Accounting:

Average salary: AU$56,153

Tax Accountants and Management Accountants are some of the jobs in this area.

Actuarial Science:

Average salary: AU$99,121

Some jobs in this area deal with financial risks in insurance and other sectors using mathematical and statistical methods.

Agricultural Science:

Salary: AU$42,000 to AU$49,000

Agriculture Scientists, Agronomists, and Forestry Consultants will fall under this category.

Architecture:

Average salary: AU$56,238

Landscape architects are in high demand in Australia.

Biomedical Engineering:

Average salary – AU$64,044

Graduate holders of this category will pave ways to treat diseases and injuries using technology.

Core Engineering:

Civil: Average salary: AU$59,282

Electrical: Average salary: AU$76,114

Mechanical: Average salary: AU$72,111

Electronics: Average salary: AU$71,450

There is a lot of demand for MS graduates in these engineering fields.

Earth sciences and related fields:

Average salary: AU$91,215

Geology, mining, and metallurgy, oil and gas engineering are some of the fields in this category.

Computer Science and IT:

Average salary – AU$75,713

Students with majors in Machine Learning, Business Intelligence, Data Visualization, and Data Management. have many job opportunities.

Psychology:

Average salary: AU$76,126

MS in clinical psychology will fall under this category.

Tourism and Hospitality Management:

Average salary: AU$83,000

Australia is a place for many tourist lovers. According to a recent survey, Australia needs 125,000 more tourist-related degree holders every year, especially accommodation and hospitality managers are in high demand.

Business Management and Data Analytics:

Salary – AU$69,161 to AU$100,000

As the number of companies opened in Australia grows yearly, jobs also increase under this category.

Medicine:

Salary – AU$75,000 to AU$95,000

Medicine and healthcare-related degrees will fall under this category.

Seeing all of these opportunities is tempting for all devoted international students. They can finish their higher education in a welcoming country that offers the best academic and personal opportunities.

Chapter 8:

Study Abroad Checklist for Singapore

Studying abroad is an enriching experience that can provide numerous benefits to students, including a unique cultural experience and a competitive edge in their education. For American students considering studying abroad, Singapore is an excellent destination that offers many advantages. One of the most surprising benefits of studying in Singapore is the affordability of higher education. Many programs offer scholarships and grants specifically for international students, and the cost of living in Singapore is lower than in other popular study-abroad destinations like the United States, the UK, and Australia.

In addition to its affordability, Singapore is an incredibly diverse and culturally rich country that attracts students from all over the world. The universities in Singapore are home to students from China, Malaysia, India, Europe, and beyond, providing ample opportunities for networking and making connections that can benefit future employment. Singapore is also a harmonious society that values cultural diversity, with a population that includes significant numbers of Hindus, Buddhists, Christians, and Muslims. Students can explore various religious sites and learn about different cultures, making their study abroad experience more meaningful and rewarding.

Singapore's economy has experienced significant growth since gaining independence in 1965, and it is now a leading center for various industries, including aerospace, engineering, information technology, pharmaceuticals, biotechnology, and more. Many multinational companies have established their headquarters in Singapore, providing additional opportunities for students to connect with potential employers.

Studying abroad in Singapore offers a unique opportunity to gain a world-class education while experiencing a diverse and welcoming culture. With its affordable tuition, cost of living, strong economy, and growing industries, Singapore is an excellent choice for American students looking to broaden their horizons and gain a competitive edge in their education and future careers.

Here are some of the top universities in Singapore.

1. National University of Singapore

The National University of Singapore (NUS), the oldest higher education institution in the country, offers a wide range of degree programs across three campuses and 16 faculties. With over 370 degrees available, including bachelor's, master's, doctoral degrees, and graduate diplomas, students have plenty of options. NUS is also home to a diverse community of students and staff from over 100 countries, creating a multicultural environment.

2. Nanyang Technological University, Singapore

Established in 1981, Nanyang Technological University, Singapore (NTU) is a well-regarded public university that focuses on research across various fields, including engineering, business, humanities, arts and social sciences, and medicine. To enhance its offerings, the university collaborates with prestigious international partners like Imperial College London to provide exceptional education to its undergraduate and graduate students. As part of this partnership, NTU has opened a new medical school to ensure its students receive the best education and training.

3. Singapore University of Technology and Design

Singapore University of Technology and Design is a renowned institution in Singapore that students worldwide are highly sought after. The university acknowledges the crucial role that arts and design play in technological and societal advancements, a fact that has been overlooked for a long time. It recognizes that these aspects are equally important as the more technical and scientific areas of study, which sets it apart from other institutions.

4. Singapore Management University

When considering a study abroad opportunity in Singapore, having multiple options is important. One highly regarded choice is Singapore Management University (SMU). Established in 2000, SMU is an independent academic institution that offers degree programs in business and computer fields and is recognized as one of the top universities in Asia. It has a diverse student population of over 12,600, with over 10% of students coming from other countries.

5. INSEAD Asia Campus

INSEAD Asia Campus is a highly-regarded institution for international students seeking higher education in Singapore. The private business school, which originated in France and is known as Institut Européen d'Administration des Affaires, has expanded its reach with a campus in Singapore since 1999. The campus offers graduate degree programs in various fields, allowing students in Asia to pursue their studies without the need to travel to the main campus in Europe. With excellent programs and facilities, INSEAD Asia Campus is a top choice for those seeking a high-quality education in Singapore.

6. Singapore University of Social Sciences

In addition to academic and research excellence, it is vital to take into account extracurricular activities, leadership involvement, and future career prospects when deciding on a university to attend. Singapore University of Social Sciences is a top-notch institution that excels in these areas, making it an ideal choice for prospective students.

7. Singapore Institute of Technology

For those aiming for swift entry into the workforce, the Singapore Institute of Technology is the ideal destination. The institution is a specialized university concentrating on practical education to create skilled professionals who contribute significantly to society's development and economic growth. SIT's degree programs are tailored to match the current requirements of different industries, guaranteeing students quality education relevant to the world of work. Engineering and business courses are among the programs provided by the university to meet society's needs, and SIT strives to satisfy this need by delivering high-quality education.

8. Nanyang Academy of Fine Arts

Nanyang Academy of Fine Arts (NAFA) is a certified higher education institution in Singapore that provides focused learning programs in Fine Arts, Design, and Music. The university offers both diploma and bachelor's degree courses to students.

9. LASALLE College of the Arts

With a mission to groom innovative and visionary artists, designers, and leaders of creative industries, LASALLE College of the Arts stands out as one of the top schools for art and design in Asia. The college offers a diverse range of undergraduate and graduate programs across various fields, including fine arts, design, media arts, and performing arts. With a strong commitment to nurturing creative talent and fostering a vibrant arts community, LASALLE has become a premier institution in Singapore, attracting students from all over the world who are passionate about pursuing a career in the arts.

10. Singapore Aviation Academy

Established in 1958, the Singapore Aviation Academy is a renowned aviation school that provides international standard training programs in aviation. As the training arm of the Civil Aviation Authority of Singapore, it offers diploma, bachelor's, and master's degree programs to equip aspiring professionals with the skills and knowledge necessary to meet the demands of the global aviation industry. The academy strives to cultivate the next generation of experts who can lead and contribute to the aviation field, and it has earned a reputation for excellence in aviation education.

Entry requirements:

Language Proficiency Requirement

In Singaporean universities, showing a good grasp of English is important. Students need to take certain tests to prove their language skills. These tests, like IELTS, TOEFL, and PTE, are a must to meet the entry requirements.

IELTS

To be eligible for undergraduate and graduate programs, a globally recognized English proficiency test, IELTS is required, with a recommended score range of 6 to 6.5 for admission to reputable universities.

TOEFL

Even though TOEFL scores are commonly used for admission to universities in North America, many universities in Singapore also use them to assess language proficiency. The minimum score required for the internet-based test is 100 or above, valid for two years.

PTE Academic

Instead of IELTS and TOEFL, PTE Academic is also an acceptable language proficiency test for students who wish to study in a foreign university. It is a computer-based exam with an average score of 68 that is required for admission.

The following 10 universities in Singapore accept PTE:

- National University of Singapore
- Nanyang Technological University
- PSB Academy
- INSEAD
- East Asia Institute of Management
- Dimensions International College
- Leadership and Management Institute
- Curtin University
- London School of Business and Finance, Singapore
- Heartpower Tesol and Teacher Training Centre

SAT (Scholarship Aptitude Test)

This is a standardized test taken by high school students who wish to enroll in an undergraduate program. It assesses their skills in reading, writing, and mathematics.

How can you pick the right program?

When selecting a university program, it is essential to consider your interests as it plays a significant role in making your university life enjoyable. Although it might not always be easy to pinpoint what you want to study, knowing your interests can make selecting suitable courses easier. Additionally, co-op or an internship is another critical factor that should be taken into account when deciding on a program. While co-op programs benefit from gaining work experience and an idea of possible careers, they might not be the best choice for everyone. Co-op programs typically take away your summers, leaving less time for leisure activities. Therefore, it is essential to consider your priorities before committing to a co-op program.

Most universities offer some hands-on learning, including experiences such as labs, field trips, student teams, study abroad, co-op and internships, studio courses, and more. Hands-on learning allows students to better understand concepts by seeing them in action. It is particularly beneficial for students who prefer to perform a task themselves. When researching universities, looking for details about experiential learning opportunities is crucial. This will allow you to filter your list of potential programs based on whether or not they offer a more traditional classroom learning style.

While studying and grades are significant aspects of university life, extracurricular activities such as residence life, sports, clubs, student government, volunteering, and more play a crucial role in your university experience. These activities provide a platform for students to socialize, build relationships, and develop new skills outside of their academic pursuits. When selecting a university, it is important to consider whether it offers activities that interest you. Some students prefer universities that provide opportunities for specific sports, while others prefer a school with extensive activity options. Therefore, it is vital to consider your extracurricular interests and the options available at potential universities.

In summary, choosing a university program requires careful consideration of your interests, co-op or internship options, experiential learning opportunities, and extracurricular activities. Considering these factors, you can find a program that meets your academic and personal goals, provides the necessary skills and knowledge, and offers an enjoyable university experience.

Scholarship options for funding:

Singapore International Graduate Award (SINGA)

The ASTAR Joint International PhD Scholarship is a collaborative scholarship offered by ASTAR, NUS, NTU, and SMU in Singapore. It provides international students pursuing a PhD in science, engineering, and technology with full tuition fee coverage, a monthly stipend, and other allowances.

President's Graduate Fellowship (PGF)

International students interested in pursuing a PhD in any field of study offered by the National University of Singapore (NUS) and the Nanyang Technological University (NTU) can apply for this scholarship. It is available exclusively to international students and offers financial support covering tuition fees, monthly stipends, and other allowances.

Monbukagakusho Research Scholarship (MEXT)

The Japanese government provides a scholarship for international students wanting to undertake graduate-level research studies in Japan. Singaporean and Singapore Permanent Residents are also eligible to apply for this scholarship.

Lee Kuan Yew Global Business Plan Competition Scholarships

The LKY-SMILE scholarship program was created in collaboration with the LKY School of Public Policy by the Singapore Management University Institute of Innovation and Entrepreneurship.

ISCA-ICAI International Scholarships

International students interested in studying accountancy in Singapore can apply for a scholarship offered jointly by the Institute of Singapore Chartered Accountants (ISCA) and the Institute of Chartered Accountants of India (ICAI).

Documents required for a Singaporean student visa:

- Passport (Original & photocopy)
- Proof of funds
- Bank statements
- Application form
- Academic marksheets
- Medical reports

- Visa application fees
- Letter of acceptance from a Singaporean university

Permanent residency (PR)/ Citizenship options:

Foreign Students Scheme

One way international students studying in Singapore can apply for permanent residence (PR) is by showcasing exceptional academic performance. However, they must have:

- resided in Singapore for more than two years
- passed any national exam like GCE 'N'/'O'/'A' levels or PSLE or are enrolled in the Integrated Program (IP).

Work Pass

Students who have completed their higher education at Singaporean universities can apply for permanent residency if they secure employment there. To be eligible for full-time work in Singapore, these graduates must obtain one of the following passes.

- Employment- passes for qualified professionals and graduates
- S -Passes for skilled foreign workers employed in Singapore.

Foreign nationals interested in becoming permanent residents of Singapore must apply through the e-PR system. Once an applicant secures a job, the employer will facilitate the application for a work pass. Non-residents must obtain a working pass to be legally employed in Singapore. However, the working pass is issued only to one employer, and if an individual switches to another company, their current working pass will be terminated, and a new application will be required. There are two types of working passes that applicants can apply for, depending on their salary. As a fresh graduate, you are most likely eligible for an 'S Pass,' while high-paying jobs can qualify for an Employment Pass.

Applicants can apply for permanent residency through the electronic Permanent Residence (e-PR) system. Once an applicant has found a job, their employer will initiate the process of applying for a working pass. A working pass is necessary for non-residents to work legally in Singapore, but it is only valid for the employer that sponsored it. If an individual changes employer, their current working pass will be revoked, and the new employer must apply for a new pass. There are two types of working passes: the 'S Pass,' which is usually required for fresh graduates, and the Employment Pass, which is reserved for high-paying jobs.

Foreign nationals must demonstrate exemplary academic performance during their stay in Singapore to qualify for permanent residency. Graduates of Singaporean higher education institutions who find employment may also be eligible for permanent residence. To obtain a working pass, an applicant's employer must meet the Ministry of Manpower's requirements, including the minimum salary threshold. The specific type of working pass will depend on an applicant's salary, qualifications, and work experience. The Employment Pass is typically reserved for highly skilled individuals in managerial, executive, or specialist roles, while the 'S Pass' is issued to mid-level qualified employees.

Students on Tuition Grant Scheme

Students who have received admission under the 'Tuition Grant Scheme' are obligated to work for a Singapore-based company for at least three years after completing their studies. On the other hand, students who are not enrolled under the Tuition Grant Scheme can choose to work for any organization, anywhere, during or after completing their degree.

Job opportunities after graduation:

Internship Programs in Singapore

Singaporean universities provide students with opportunities to gain practical experience in their field of study through "Industrial

Attachment" or internships. These internships are either mandatory or optional components of the course module. Students will receive valuable practical experience related to their area of study. The length of the internships usually lasts for 5 to 6 months, and most of them are paid. However, the stipend amount may vary depending on the program.

Teaching jobs

Fluency in English can be an advantage for those seeking teaching jobs in Singapore since it is the primary language used for education. A TEFL qualification is necessary for teaching in public schools. The requirements for eligibility may vary depending on the company or institution offering the teaching position.

Doctors/ Physician/ Nursing

Doctoral program graduates in Singapore are among the highest-paid professionals, with careers such as nursing, physician practices, physiotherapy, and physician specialties. The average salary for these professionals ranges from 15,100 SGD to 43,500 SGD, making it one of the highest-paying career paths in Singapore.

Engineering/ IT/ Data Analytics

Among international students, engineering and data scientists are highly sought after. The average salary offered to individuals in this field ranges from 7,920 to 14,500 SGD monthly.

Pilots

Piloting is a profession that involves taking care of passengers during flights. This job requires intensive training and a high level of responsibility. The average salary offered to pilots ranges from 6,030 SGD to 19,700 SGD.

College Professors

Becoming a college professor is a career that demands perseverance and endurance. It involves a comprehensive approach. The average salary range for this profession is 7,240 SGD to 23,700 SGD.

Orthodontists

Orthodontics is highly lucrative as it deals with dental services, and people are willing to pay more for good quality service. Orthodontists earn an average salary ranging from 8,150 SGD to 26,600 SGD.

Chapter 9:

Study Abroad Checklist for Dubai, UAE

Dubai, United Arab Emirates (UAE), is renowned for its towering skyscrapers and picturesque skyline, but it also boasts a remarkable education system that places a high value on research and innovation. Education is a top priority for the city, evident in its provision of high-quality and accessible education for its residents.

Dubai's education system offers a wide range of degree programs through its internationally recognized universities and colleges. With a diverse selection of schools, pre-schools, colleges, and universities that cater to varying price points and amenities, Dubai's educational infrastructure can accommodate the learning needs of children from a young age. The city's schools offer an array of curricula, including the UK National Curriculum, IB, CBSE, GCSE, IGSCE, Montessori, Cambridge, French, Australian, UAE MoE, Chinese, and Iranian curriculums.

A good education is often a gateway to a good job, and considering Dubai's thriving economy - ranked the 5th-largest in the Middle

East - provides a wealth of employment opportunities across various industries, including finance, tourism, and healthcare. The job market in Dubai has expanded to new levels, with multiple foreign companies setting up branches in the city. In addition, jobs related to technology and artificial intelligence are said to have a high scope in the region, making Dubai an ideal destination for those seeking a career in these fields.

As Dubai continues to grow and develop, the city is projected to offer unparalleled career opportunities to graduates in areas such as Artificial Intelligence, Data Sciences, HR, Business Studies, Financial Analysis, Engineering, and more. Dubai is the city for you if you want to shape your career and secure high-paying, future-proof employment opportunities.

Top universities in Dubai:

1. Al Ghurair University (AGU):

Al Ghurair University is a private university located within the Dubai International Academic City (DIAC), established with the mission of imparting knowledge and skills to students to help them contribute towards the progress and productivity of their communities. The university is licensed by the Ministry of Education, Higher Education Affairs (MOHESR) and offers bachelor's degree programs across its three colleges. These colleges are the University of Dubai (UD), Zayed University, and Biotechnology University College Dubai (BUC).

2. The University of Dubai

The University of Dubai is a globally and nationally accredited university in the heart of Dubai. The university was set up to bridge the skills gap in the workforce, and today it offers undergraduate degree programs in a wide range of subjects, including business administration, management, marketing, finance, banking, accounting, human resources management, entrepreneurship management, economics, supply chain and logistics management, and information technology.

3. Zayed University

Zayed University is the latest among the three government-sponsored universities in the UAE, with three main campuses - one in Abu Dhabi and two in Dubai. Six colleges offer globally recognized undergraduate and postgraduate degrees in arts, business, communication and media sciences, education, sustainable sciences and humanities, and technological innovation.

4. Biotechnology University College Dubai (BUC)

Biotechnology University College Dubai (BUC) is a MOHESR-accredited biotechnology institution that provides undergraduate and postgraduate programs in biotechnology, medical and pharmaceutical studies, environmental and agricultural studies, and petroleum and industrial studies.

5. The Higher Colleges of Technology (HCT)

The Higher Colleges of Technology (HCT) is one of the largest institutions of higher learning in the UAE, with over 55,000 UAE nationals as graduates. The HCT has 17 campuses, including two in Dubai, namely the Dubai Men's College (DMC) and Dubai Women's College (DWC), offering undergraduate programs in business.

6. The American University in Dubai (AUD)

The American University in Dubai (AUD) is a private university situated in Dubai next to Dubai Media City, Dubai Internet City, and the Palm Islands. It started as a branch campus of the American InterContinental University in Atlanta, Georgia (US). The AUD has both US (SACSCOC) and UAE (MOHESR) accreditations and offers a variety of undergraduate and postgraduate programs, including finance and accounting, business and management, engineering and information studies, and arts and humanities (the latter exclusively as a postgraduate program).

7. The University of Wollongong in Dubai (UOWD)

The University of Wollongong in Dubai (UOWD) is a private university located in the Dubai Knowledge Village, founded as a branch campus of the University of Wollongong in Australia in 1993. UOWD offers a range of undergraduate and postgraduate programs, including finance and accounting, business and management, engineering and information studies, and arts and humanities (the latter exclusively as a postgraduate program).

8. The British University in Dubai (BUiD)

The British University in Dubai (BUiD) is a research-based postgraduate university that collaborates with multiple leading UK universities, such as the University of Edinburgh, the University of Manchester, Cardiff University, and King's College London. BUiD is situated in the Dubai International Academic City and offers MOHESR-accredited programs in business administration (MBA), informatics, and information technology management.

9. The American University in the Emirates (AUE)

The American University in the Emirates (AUE) is a private university licensed by the CAA and located in the Dubai International Academic City. AUE operates and collaborates with several US and international universities and offers undergraduate and graduate programs, excluding PhD programs.

Dubai boasts a rich and diverse educational infrastructure featuring a range of internationally accredited institutions offering undergraduate and postgraduate programs across various disciplines. These universities and colleges are equipped with modern facilities and experienced faculty dedicated to ensuring students receive a high-quality education. Graduates of these institutions are well-equipped to contribute positively to their communities and take up high.

Requirements for admission:

- completed application form
- proof of paying the application fee (if applicable)
- high school diploma (to apply for a Bachelor's)

- Bachelor's diploma (to apply for a Master's)
- transcript of records
- passport-sized photo(s)
- copy of valid passport and/or personal ID
- motivation letter.

How to find the right program:

It is essential for students to carefully consider the impact that their chosen study program can have on their future after college. Before enrolling in a degree program, it is crucial to research the university, its teaching methods, and the employability prospects it offers. Students should consider factors such as global ranking, recognition, international partnerships, and a research-based curriculum when making their final decision.

While some students have a clear idea of their desired major, others may not dedicate enough time to contemplate their options, leading them down an unsuitable career path. To ensure a fulfilling university experience, students should choose a school that aligns with their educational and career goals.

As students return to physical classrooms, blended learning will become integral to post-pandemic education. Therefore, students need to confirm that their chosen university has the necessary infrastructure to support online learning and provide a well-rounded educational experience. In today's context, a strong technological infrastructure is crucial for any degree program. Students should also evaluate the university's flexibility in offering programs in a blended, face-to-face, or online mode before enrolling.

Scholarships in Dubai:

Several organizations in the UAE offer scholarships to students pursuing undergraduate or postgraduate studies in specialized fields. These scholarships help students achieve their academic goals and contribute to the country's economic growth and development.

The Masaar Scholarship

The Masaar Scholarship, offered by the Ministry of Finance and The Federal Authority for Government Human Resources, is aimed at providing financial aid to students pursuing their studies in finance and accounting. The scholarship program is intended to help students gain scientific qualifications, which can aid them in getting employed at the Ministry of Finance after completing their course. Eligibility criteria for the program include obtaining a high school certificate or equivalent with an average grade of no less than 75% or a cumulative average of no less than 3%. Additionally, students must have graduated from high school within the past three years, not be employed, and not be combining multiple scholarships.

The Emirates Nuclear Energy Corporation (ENEC)

The Emirates Nuclear Energy Corporation (ENEC) also offers a scholarship program for talented Emirati students pursuing Bachelor's or Master's degrees in Nuclear Engineering. The scholarship is offered in partnership with Abu Dhabi Polytechnic, providing students with opportunities to gain professional experience and interact with specialists in the field. To apply for the program, students must be UAE nationals, not over 22 years of age, high school graduates in the Advanced Track with a minimum average grade of 80%, and earn a score of 5.5 or equivalent in the English proficiency test (IELTS).

Abu Dhabi National Oil Company (ADNOC) Scholarship Program

ADNOC offers scholarships in engineering, artificial intelligence, finance management, and economics, among other fields, locally and internationally. The scholarships are designed to encourage students to pursue their studies and support the country's economic and industrial objectives. To be eligible, students must pass an interview with the ADNOC Scholarship Department, be medically fit, and obtain a military service release letter if applicable.

The ICT Fund's BETHA program

The ICT Fund's BETHA program supports Emirati students pursuing computer engineering, electronic engineering, computer science, and information technology. This program enables students to study in countries like the USA, UK, Australia, Japan, and the UAE. The ICT Fund aims to set industry standards globally and is committed to making fast, innovative, and stable changes to the ICT sector.

The Full Tuition Scholarship

The Full Tuition Scholarship is granted to undergraduate students who demonstrate excellent academic performance and maintain it throughout their studies at UAEU. It provides full financial support by waiving 100% of the tuition fees for eligible students.

UAE University offers partial tuition scholarships of up to 50% to exceptional high school graduates as an incentive scholarship during their university studies. The scholarships are available to students in various colleges except for the College of Law, the Literary track in the College of Education, Arabic Programs in the College of Humanities and Social Sciences, and the College of Business and Economics. To be eligible, students must have a minimum score of 90% in their Grade 12 certificate or its equivalent, meet English language proficiency requirements of IELTS 6.5 or its equivalent, and score at least 630 in the Math SAT Subject Test (level 2) or at least 1400 in the Math Em SAT or its equivalent.

These scholarships offer excellent opportunities for students to achieve their academic goals in specialized fields and contribute to the UAE's economic growth and development. The eligibility criteria for each scholarship vary, and students are advised to check the requirements carefully before applying.

Student eligibility criteria for applications:

To be eligible for admission to UAEU and receive financial aid, students must meet specific academic requirements. These include a minimum score of 97% on their high school certificate or equivalent, as well as a score of at least seven on the IELTS English proficiency exam or a score of 1675 on the EmSAT English exam. In addition, students must achieve a minimum score of 680 on the Math SAT Subject Test (level 2) or 1500 on the Math EmSAT exam unless they apply to specific colleges. Students must achieve a different minimum score for admission to the College of Law, the Literary track in the College of Education, Arabic Programs in the College of Humanities and Social Sciences, and the College of Business and Economics. Finally, students seeking admission to the College of Law, the Literary track in the College of Education, and Arabic Programs in the College of Humanities and Social Sciences must obtain a minimum score of 1350 on the EmSAT Arabic exam or its equivalent.

Documents required for admission:

- Student's Birth Certificate
- Parent's Passports
- Parents' Residency Visas*
- Parent's Emirates IDs*
- Student's Emirates ID
- Student's Photo (Passport Size)
- Parents' Photo (Passport Size)
- Copy of a valid UAE Residence Visa.
- Previous Schengen, USA, or UK visa copy;
- Declaration of Value (or Statement of Comparability released by CIMEA);
- Pre-enrolment letter released by the UNIVERSITALY portal, or enrolment letter if in pre-enrolment is not required;
- Copy of the final academic qualification duly attested and apostilled.
- Proof of sufficient means of subsistence. A minimum of € 45

Permanent residency and extended visa options:

Student visa

International students can reside in the UAE for their studies either under the sponsorship of their parent, a UAE resident, or the university they are studying at. The university's student affairs department can assist in obtaining a student visa, which is valid for one year and renewable upon submission of proof of continuing studies. Family members of foreign students can also stay in the UAE as long as they can provide suitable housing. This initiative by the government aims to promote moral stability for the students. To be eligible for a UAE residence visa, individuals must fall under one of the categories outlined by the government:

- You will work in the UAE, under a governmental office, or in a private company.
- You will study in a UAE educational institution.
- You are the dependent of a UAE citizen or foreign resident (child, parent, maid, or a close relative)
- You have made an investment in the UAE
- You have purchased the property in the UAE
- You will retire in the UAE

Types of UAE Residence Visas

Residence visas in the UAE are categorized based on the purpose of the individual's visit. There are various types of tickets available, including a Work Visa for those who have secured employment in the UAE and obtained a Work Permit, a Student Visa for foreign nationals who have been accepted into a UAE educational institution, a Family Visa for those close family members of UAE citizens or foreign residents, an Investment Visa (long-term residence) for those who make a substantial investment in the UAE, and a Retirement Visa for elderly foreigners who wish to retire in the UAE and have the financial means to do so. Additionally, a program called "Work Remotely from Dubai" provides visas to foreign freelancers who want to work remotely in Dubai.

Job opportunities in Dubai:

Various employment opportunities are available for UAE students based on their skills and interests. The job options for students are not limited to but may include the following:

- Graphic design jobs
- Social Media expert jobs
- Content writing and development jobs
- Medical assistant jobs
- Translators
- Tour guides
- Restaurant servers and waiters
- Laundry and cleaning services
- Home tutoring jobs
- Substitute teacher roles
- Online jobs
- Sales management and monitoring jobs

Apart from these, various part-time job options are available depending on a student's skills and interests. One potential job opportunity for bilingual students is translation work. Freelance translation work is available through platforms like MotaWord or Gengo or organizations like universities and banks. The most commonly used languages for translation services in Dubai are English and Arabic, and students can expect to earn around 4,000 AED per month. The benefits of this job include flexible hours, excellent pay, and valuable work experience for a resume.

Another part-time job option for students in the UAE is working as a call center worker. While this job may involve more mundane tasks like cold-calling people for marketing purposes or providing business customer support, it can offer good pay and benefits. International students who speak English may find call Centre jobs particularly appealing, and the minimum requirements typically include call center experience, language skills, and customer service skills. Students can expect to earn between 2,000 to 3,500 AED per month working in a call center. Some companies that offer call center jobs in the UAE include Oasis Group, AFIA Insurance, and Parker Connect.

Overall, many job opportunities are available for students in the UAE, and it's important for students to consider their skills and interests when searching for part-time work. Translation and call center jobs are just two examples of the many options available, and they can offer good pay, flexible hours, and valuable work experience. By exploring different job options and applying to companies that match their skills and interests, students in the UAE can find part-time work that helps them support their education and build their resumes.

Chapter 10:
Study Abroad Checklist for Denmark

Denmark boasts a wealth of high-quality educational opportunities, with five Danish universities ranking among the top institutions globally according to QS World University Ranking. The degrees earned at Danish universities and colleges are internationally recognized and offer valuable preparation for future career prospects.

Contrary to popular belief, studying in Denmark is not prohibitively expensive. Tuition fees vary depending on the level and duration of the education, with the most affordable degree programs starting from just 6,000 EUR per year. Additionally, scholarships are often available to students based on merit, with universities seeking the most accomplished applicants who can contribute to their academic standards.

The Erasmus Mundus Scholarship Program is a great opportunity for students from inside and outside the EU who aim to get a master's or doctoral degree. This program, funded by the European Union, covers everything - from tuition fees to travel and insurance. Plus, it provides a monthly allowance for day-to-day living expenses.

Applicants with exceptional academic backgrounds and strong English language proficiency are encouraged to apply.

The Danish higher education system is widely recognized for its innovative approach and exceptional academic standards across various study subjects. The universities in Denmark frequently engage in partnerships with businesses, industries, and research institutes, which fosters a dynamic learning environment that allows students to learn directly from industry experts. Additionally, many programs offer credit-earning internships to provide students with valuable work experience.

Collaborative teamwork and inspiration are fundamental values that are deeply embedded in the Danish education system. Students are encouraged or required to work in groups throughout their studies, including during exams and thesis work. The higher education system in Denmark blends traditional lectures and tutorials with innovative teaching methods that help students develop strong problem-solving skills.

Problem-based learning methods and open debate encourage students to express themselves, pursue experimentation, and collaborate with others. The learning environment in Denmark is welcoming and relaxed, with students and teachers openly discussing ideas during class and lectures.

Studying in Denmark also offers a welcoming and open-minded environment for international students. With a diverse student population from around the world, there are ample opportunities to build valuable networks and engage with different cultures. Furthermore, Denmark is considered a safe and tolerant country, where instances of racism are rare. While Danish is the primary language spoken in the country, 70% of the population is fluent in English, making communication easy for international students.

Denmark also offers a wealth of leisure and entertainment options, including libraries, restaurants, and outdoor activities. The country has a reputation as one of the happiest nations globally due in no small part to the positive attitude of the Danish people. Regular social events and community gatherings offer a chance for people to come together and enjoy life outside of work and study.

Finally, healthcare facilities in Denmark are widely available and affordable. This means that international students can enjoy peace of mind knowing they will have access to medical care if needed. These factors make Denmark an attractive destination for students seeking a high-quality education in a welcoming and enjoyable environment.

Top 10 Universities in Denmark

1. University of Copenhagen

Ranked 76th in the world and Denmark's top university, the University of Copenhagen, one of Europe's oldest institutions, was founded in 1479. The university prides itself on research-based teaching and a perfect faculty-student ratio score. With 39,000 students, the University of Copenhagen is committed to sustainability and is one of the world's greenest campuses.

2. Technical University of Denmark

The Technical University of Denmark (DTU) has risen nine places to 103rd in the world rankings this year, performing well in most of the indicators. The university aims to develop and create value using natural sciences and technical science, particularly excelling in its Environmental Science course, ranking 45th worldwide in 2020. DTU is known for attracting and retaining excellent faculty members, reflected in its student-faculty ratio ranking 25th in the world and its international faculty ranking 62nd.

3. Aarhus University

Aarhus University falls two places in the 2020 world rankings to 147th but still boasts an impressive ranking. Around 12 percent of its 40,000 students are international, representing over 120 nationalities. Aarhus University is renowned for its research output, particularly in Archaeology, where it places 27th in the world in the QS World

University Rankings by Subject 2020. The university focuses on research-based learning and is committed to providing a welcoming environment for international students.

4. Aalborg University

Aalborg University climbed an incredible 19 places in the 2020 world rankings to joint 305th. This year, the university's highest scores are for the international faculty indicator, and 15 percent of its students are international. Aalborg University offers a real-world approach to learning backed up by world-class research. It has campuses in several Danish cities, including Aalborg, Esbjerg, and Copenhagen.

5. University of Southern Denmark

Ranked joint 353rd in the world, the University of Southern Denmark has risen four places in the 2020 world rankings. The university's highest score is in the international students indicator, with one in five students coming from outside Denmark. The University of Southern Denmark focuses on developing transferrable skills that can be used in various industries, offering campuses in several cities across Denmark.

6. Copenhagen Business School

Copenhagen Business School (CBS) offers an excellent academic and research environment alongside extracurricular activities, leadership participation, and career opportunities. It is the perfect training ground for students who want to pursue a career in the business industry. CBS boasts professionals and educators with deep experience in the actual field, and its curriculum includes rigorous assessments and practical training that help students create ways to face challenges in the business community.

7. Roskilde University

Roskilde University was established to disseminate knowledge in new ways and has become the epitome of academic excellence and inclusive education. The university offers transparency and democracy in knowledge-sharing, contributing to society through innovative and experimental research activities.

8. IT University of Copenhagen

The IT University of Copenhagen was established to deliver state-of-the-art digital design, computer science, and information technology education. It creates profound knowledge in the industry that paves the way for the development of groundbreaking technology that benefits humanity. The university collaborates with various public sectors and international researchers to ignite the strong entrepreneurial spirit of its students.

9. Royal Danish Academy - Education with a Social Mission

The Royal Danish Academy of Architecture, Design, and Conservation was established to develop students who can bring about positive societal changes through their skills and talents. The academy employs a productive teaching strategy that enables students to become professionals in their respective fields. Additionally, the academy fosters an inclusive academic community where students and staff can collaborate to create a more equitable and valuable world.

10. University College Lillebaelt - Large Institution with Global Reach

With over 11,000 students spread across its campuses, University College Lillebaelt is the seventh-largest educational institution in Denmark. The university offers various courses and programs and is open to exchange students worldwide. It aims to become a hub for growth and welfare and develop solutions that can significantly impact society.

Entry Requirements

To get into a Danish college, your education needs to be on par with what Danish students learn in high school before they graduate. However, a relevant vocational qualification may be sufficient for specific programs, such as Academy Profession degree programs.

In addition to meeting the general requirements, you must also fulfill the specific requirements for the individual study program, which may include subject level, grades, and overall average marks. You should consult the institution's website to check for specific requirements.

If you do not meet the criteria, you may be able to take supplementary courses but note that they are only available in Danish and will not improve your GPA score. Language proficiency in Danish or English may also be necessary for some programs, and you must meet these requirements before the program starts.

Application Process:

You can begin the application process once you meet the qualifications and requirements. It is recommended to start early and allow ample time to obtain all the necessary documents. The application for undergraduate higher education is centrally coordinated but evaluated locally by the institutions. As a result, you do not apply directly to a single institution.

You can apply for up to 8 programs simultaneously, but you will receive only one offer for admission (if any), which will be at the highest priority program. You must print and sign a signature page generated on www.optagelse.dk for each program you apply to, containing an application ID, which the higher education institution needs to locate and download your application.

If you apply for multiple programs at the same institution, you will need to send multiple signature pages by mail or email after printing and signing them by hand. Diplomas and other documents should be uploaded on www.optagelse.dk according to the deadlines and requirements specified by the institutions. You can change your applications, including the order of priority and deletion of applications, before 5 July at 12 PM on www.optagelse.dk.

Picking The Right Program

Choosing a university program can be challenging, especially when you're unsure what you want to study. While your interests are a crucial factor to consider, hands-on learning can also significantly make your university experience more enjoyable and fulfilling.

Many universities offer experiential learning opportunities, such as labs, field trips, internships, and study abroad programs, which can help you understand complex concepts better. Therefore, when researching universities, check their hands-on learning options, as this can help you determine which programs align with your learning preferences.

Additionally, it's essential to consider the type of degree you'll earn upon graduation, as programs with the same name can differ significantly between universities. To narrow your search, look for universities offering courses that align with your interests and goals. Also, check the required courses for the programs you're considering to gain valuable insights into what you'll learn.

When financing your education, having a budget in mind is crucial, as university costs can be high, and you're likely to pay a significant portion yourself. Research if the universities you're considering offer paid co-op or internship programs to help cover your expenses. However, remember that your potential contributions and skills are typically more important to employers than the name of your degree.

When selecting a university program, consider your interests, preferred learning style, and the type of degree you'll earn upon graduation. Research the required courses for the programs you're considering and investigate financing options to determine the best fit for you.

Scholarships

1. Nordplus Program for International Students in Denmark

The Nordplus program is a well-known scholarship offered to international students at Nordic institutions in Denmark. It is available for undergraduate, postgraduate, and doctoral-level studies at partner universities and institutions.

2. Erasmus program for Higher Education in Denmark and Europe

The Erasmus program is a highly popular scholarship for students pursuing bachelor's, master's, and doctoral degree programs across Europe, including Denmark. The application for this scholarship can be made through a Danish university.

3. Erasmus Mundus/Joint Master Degree program for International Students

The Erasmus Mundus program provides complete funding for international students pursuing their master's degree programs in Denmark. It is specifically available for specific Erasmus Mundus Joint Master degree courses at select universities and is a top choice for Indian students.

4. Government Scholarships for UG, PG, and PhD Studies in Denmark

The Denmark government scholarship is a significant scholarship available for international students pursuing undergraduate, postgraduate, and doctoral degree programs in Denmark. It is supported by the Ministry of Higher Education and Science and can be obtained through one of the eight universities in Denmark.

5. Berklee on the Road Clinics Scholarship for Music Education

Berklee College of Music provides institutional aid to 40% of incoming students, with an average award covering 40% of tuition. The college also offers teaching and performance programs across various locations in the United States and the world, such as Los Angeles, Puerto Rico, Ireland, Italy, and Japan. The Berklee on the Road Clinics scholarship is available to students based on their performance during these programs.

6. 6G Excellence Scholarships for Master's Program in Intelligent Communication Systems

EURECOM and the OpenAirInterface Software Alliance have collaborated to create the 6G Excellence scholarship program. It is available for highly motivated students to pursue a Master of Science in Intelligent Communication Systems.

7. Drs. Anthony and Joanne Edmonds Study Abroad Scholarship for History Students

The Edmonds Scholarship provides financial assistance to a Department of History student preparing to study abroad every odd year. This scholarship alternates between the Department of History and the Honors College. Drs. Anthony and Joanne Edmonds have dedicated more than 60 years to Ball State and the Honors College and encouraged study-abroad experiences for students.

8. Spreadsheet Gladiator Scholarship for Business, Computer Science, or Communications Students

Spreadsheets are used by over 2 billion people worldwide in their daily tasks, including in their careers. To recognize those entering the business field, Coefficient offers an annual $1,500 scholarship to a college student pursuing a degree in Business, Computer Science, or Communications.

9. Pinsky Law New Venture Development Scholarship for Entrepreneurs and Startups

Pinsky Law provides its services to entrepreneurs and startup companies, and they have developed and maintained the legal resources for startups section on their website. They understand that establishing and operating a new venture is challenging and requires a significant financial commitment. Therefore, they offer the Pinsky Law New Venture Development Scholarship to support aspiring entrepreneurs.

Visa Process

To apply for a study permit in Denmark, you must first accept a place at an accredited Danish institution and pay an application fee. You must then gather all required documents, including a formal letter of admission, academic program details, passport, and photos, completed ST1 form, language proficiency proof, evidence of financial resources, living arrangements, application fee payment receipt, and travel insurance proof.

You must also have your biometric data recorded at a Danish diplomatic mission, application center, or police station within 14 days of submission. The processing time for a Danish student visa is typically two months, but it may take longer for certain nationalities, such as students from Nigeria, Pakistan, Kenya, and Ghana. It's essential to plan and allow for sufficient time to process your application.

PR

There are several requirements that you must meet to qualify for permanent residency in Denmark. Firstly, you must be over the age of 18. You must still meet the needs for your current residence permit and be a resident in Denmark when the immigration services decide on your residence permit application. If, for any reason, you are outside of Denmark, you must return to the country.

You need to have been a legal resident of Denmark for at least eight uninterrupted years when the immigration service decides on the residence application. It is important to note that if you have been convicted of certain crimes and sentenced to more than six months, you will be ineligible for a permanent residence permit.

You cannot qualify for a residence permit if you have overdue payments for the Social Service Act or active Social Policy Act benefits, child support paid in advance, daycare payments, overpaid housing benefits, housing subsidy loans, taxes, and levies.

You must not have received certain forms of social benefits within four years of applying for a permanent residence permit or until the permanent residence permit is granted. It is also a requirement to accept a declaration of residence and self-support, which is included in the application both online and in printable form.

To be eligible for permanent residency, you must be employed. It would be best if you had a job at the time the Immigration Service decides on your application. The requirements for employment are that you must be employed in a non-terminated, permanent position, and you can prove that you will continue to be employed or are self-employed. It is also essential not to have worked against establishing your identity.

This can include presenting falsified identity documents another person's identity document, or giving false information about your data, such as your name, date of birth, country of birth, or citizenship.

You must pass the Danish language test 2 or a Danish exam of an equal or higher level, such as the FVU reading exam (level 2 or 3) or any exam considered equivalent or higher than Prøve i Dansk 3.

You need to have been employed for at least three years and six months. The following types of employment can be considered as regular employment: paid employment (minimum 30 hours per week, or 120 hours per month), work as a self-employed if the work carries the same weight as regular full-time employment, working for a business owned by your spouse, sick leave, holiday, absence to care for family members and parental leave, etc. within the terms and conditions of your employment.

Flexjob can also be considered if it meets the terms established by the Active Employment Policy Act. To be eligible for permanent residency in Denmark, you must fulfill all the abovementioned requirements. This includes being over the age of 18, meeting the legal requirements for your current residence permit, having eight years of lawful residency in Denmark, not being convicted of certain crimes, having no overdue public debts, not receiving certain forms of social benefits, accepting a declaration of residence and self-support, being employed, not working against the establishment of your identity, passing the Danish language test 2, and having been employed for at least three years and six months.

Job Opportunities

Denmark has a strong and diverse economy with a low unemployment rate of 2.7%. The country's location makes it an important distribution point for Europe, and its top exports include pharmaceuticals, medical equipment, iron and steel, food products, textiles, clothing, and electronics.

The Danish labor market operates on a system of 'flexicurity,' which allows employers to adapt to the market's needs by hiring and firing at will while employees are protected by A-kasse (unemployment insurance fund).

The working conditions in Denmark are exceptional, with strong collaboration between unions, employers, and the government and a focus on small and medium-sized enterprises. Some of the world's most famous brands, such as Pandora, Carlsberg, Ecco, and Lego, have their roots in Denmark. Graduates have many job opportunities in Denmark, with popular jobs including mechanical engineers, radiographers, IT consultants, primary and secondary school teachers, and psychologists.

Chapter 11:

Study Abroad Checklist for the Netherlands

The Netherlands boasts one of the world's oldest and most prestigious higher education systems, with numerous universities consistently ranking highly globally. As a result, studying abroad in the Netherlands has become a popular choice for many international students, especially from underdeveloped and developing countries, who can benefit from the country's welcoming and inclusive environment, economical tuition fees, and extensive range of English-language programs.

Dutch society is known for its "live and let live" approach, reflecting the people's diverse and accepting atmosphere. This inclusiveness has long been a core value of Dutch culture and is another factor that contributes to the Netherlands' appeal as a study-abroad destination.

Graduates of Dutch universities often wish to stay in the country because of its robust economy, financial growth, and job opportunities.

The Netherlands is a thriving tech and startup hub, and the government actively encourages innovation and the recruitment of skilled foreign workers, resulting in an assorted and dynamic workforce.

Top Universities in the Netherlands.

1. Wageningen University & Research (WUR)

Specializing in agricultural and environmental sciences, Wageningen University & Research offers a variety of undergraduate and postgraduate programs in Dutch and English. With over 27% of its student body coming from overseas, it is a popular choice for international students.

2. University of Amsterdam (UoA)

Founded in 1632, the University of Amsterdam is the country's third oldest and the largest institution in the Netherlands. It is highly regarded for its arts and humanities and social sciences programs, worldwidem all over the world.

3. Utrecht University

Established in 1636, Utrecht University is a prominent research university with students and staff of 118 different nationalities. It is one of the largest universities in the Netherlands and offers a wide range of academic programs.

4. Delft University of Technology (DUT)

Delft University of Technology is the country's largest and oldest public technical university. It was established as a royal academy for civil engineers, and it is known for its engineering and technology programs.

5. University of Groningen

Inaugurated in 1614, the University of Groningen offers a diverse range of English-taught bachelor's and master's degrees across 11 faculties and nine graduate schools. It is located in the city of Groningen.

6. Leiden University

Founded in 1575 as a Protestant university, Leiden University is a public research institution in Leiden. It is one of the oldest universities in the Netherlands and is regarded highly for its research and academic programs.

7. Erasmus University College

Erasmus University College is a public liberal arts college located in Rotterdam. It is the undergraduate honors college of the Erasmus University Rotterdam, offering a BSc degree in Liberal Arts & Sciences.

8. Radboud University Nijmegen

Located in Nijmegen, Radboud University is a public research university named after Saint Radboud, a 9th-century Dutch bishop known for his intellect and support of the underprivileged.

9. Vrije Universiteit Amsterdam

Founded in 1880, Vrije Universiteit Amsterdam is a public research university offering a range of academic programs. It is one of the two largest, publicly funded research universities in Amsterdam.

10. Maastricht University

Established in 1976, Maastricht University is the second youngest of the 13 Dutch universities. It has a diverse student population, with over 56% of its students coming from abroad.

Entry Requirements

Admission requirements for higher education programs in the Netherlands are usually set by the educational institution and typically require a certain level of qualification. To determine if your diploma meets the minimum requirements for your desired program, you can compare your qualifications with those listed on the Nuffic website. Nuffic can also guide to educational institutions regarding the evaluation of foreign qualifications.

Proficiency in the English language is crucial, and applicants must pass an English language test, with commonly accepted tests being the IELTS and TOEFL. However, institutions may accept other tests, such as Cambridge English. The required scores for TOEFL are a minimum of 550 (paper-based) or 213 (internet-based), and for IELTS, a minimum average of 6.

In some cases, applicants may not be eligible for their desired program, but they may succeed the following year with extra preparation. In such cases, the university's international office should be contacted to determine if the applicant's degree is recognized in the Netherlands. Additionally, applicants may need a residence permit if they are not an EU/EEA or Swiss citizen, a good command of Dutch if they are pursuing a program taught in Dutch, and a minimum average of 7-7.5 for foreign diplomas.

It is also important to note that admission requirements vary depending on the university and subject of interest, and for some programs, a selection procedure takes place due to a larger number of applicants than available seats.

Finding the right program

When choosing between a university of applied sciences and a research university, consider your career goals and the type of education that suits you best. If you aspire to work in an applied profession such as engineering, IT, logistics management, or travel management, a university of applied sciences may be the right choice. These universities provide practical training that prepares you for the workforce and may offer opportunities for internships that could lead to job offers.

On the other hand, if you're interested in scientific research or teaching, a research university may be more suitable. Dutch research universities have produced numerous Nobel and other prestigious prize winners and contributed to significant scientific discoveries that have positively impacted human life. To determine the reputation and achievements of a research university you're interested in, consult international university rankings that showcase the best universities in the world.

When choosing a university based on its ranking, remember that the higher the rank, the more challenging and rigorous the education may be. Also, a university may not have the highest overall ranking but may be a leader in your area of interest. For instance, Tilburg University is ranked 357th overall by QS, but it is highly regarded for its business and management programs, ranking 50th in QS Economics and Econometrics.

It's essential to communicate with representatives of the universities you're interested in to learn about their specific modes of delivering content to students. Determine whether the industry you want to enter requires a strong foundation in theoretical knowledge or values industry experience. For example, becoming a dentist requires practical experience in a clinical setting to prepare you for different medical conditions you may encounter.

Identify the key factors you want in a course, such as the duration of the program, whether you can earn credits for your existing experience, the skills you want to learn, and whether work experience is essential to you. This will help you in making an informed decision when choosing the right university for your goals.

Scholarships and Funding

1. Orange Knowledge Program

The Orange Knowledge Program is designed to enhance the capacity, knowledge, and quality of individuals and organizations in higher and vocational education and other fields related to priority themes in participating countries.

2. University of Twente Scholarships (UTS)

The University of Twente Scholarships are available for outstanding students from EU/EEA and non-EU/EEA countries who apply for a graduate program (MSc) at the University of Twente.

3. Leiden University Excellence Scholarships (LexS)

Leiden University Excellence Scholarships are awarded to exceptional non-EEA and non-EFTA students who are enrolled in a full-time master's degree program at Leiden University.

4. Holland Scholarship for Non-EEA International Students

The Holland Scholarship is funded by the Dutch Ministry of Education, Culture, and Science. It is intended for international students from outside the European Economic Area (EEA) who wish to pursue a bachelor's or master's degree at one of the Dutch research universities or universities of applied sciences in Holland.

5. Utrecht Excellence Scholarships for International Students

The Utrecht Excellence Scholarship provides an opportunity, especially for international students from outside the EEA to pursue a master's degree in selected fields at Utrecht University.

6. VU Amsterdam Fellowship Program for International Students

The VU Fellowship Program offers talented prospective non-EU/ EEA students a unique chance to pursue a master's degree at Vrije Universiteit Amsterdam.

7. Maastricht University Holland High Potential Scholarships for International Students

Maastricht University offers the Holland-High Potential Scholarship to highly talented students from outside the European Union (EU) who have been admitted to a master's program at UM. The scholarship includes a tuition fee waiver, a monthly stipend, and a Holland Scholarship.

PR Requirements

General requirements that apply to all individuals must be fulfilled.

- A valid Dutch residence permit must have been held for at least five consecutive years, with some exceptions to the five years.
- For children, only those aged at least 13 years old and with a valid residence permit from the age of 8 can apply for a permanent residence permit. Moreover, only years from age 8 onwards will count towards the five years.
- During the entire 5-year period, the main residence should have been in the Netherlands.
- The residence permit should have always been extended on time, and the requirements for the permit should have been met and still met.
- The government must currently give a valid non-temporary residence permit.
- The individual should not pose a threat to public order or national security.
- No incorrect or incomplete information should have been provided while applying for the current residence permit, which, with the correct information, would have been rejected.
- The income criterion should be fulfilled.
- Registration in the Personal Records Database (BRP) at the local town hall is necessary.
- Civic integration examination must have been passed, or it may not be necessary to take the exam.
- If the applicant was born in the Netherlands and is now 18 years old or under three years old when they started living in the Netherlands and have always lived there since then, the IND can only reject their application if they pose a threat to public order or national security.

In the case of applying for a permanent residence permit, the requirements for the residence permit for a long-term EU resident will be checked first by the IND. No action is required from the applicant's side.

Having a residence permit for a long-term EU resident will make it easier to apply for a residence permit in another EU country, but the permit requirements in that country still need to be met.

Job Opportunities

The Netherlands has become an attractive destination for expats seeking professional development and a high quality of life. Although salaries may be lower than in some other countries, the opportunity to build a successful career is still available. The country's largest cities, such as Amsterdam and Rotterdam, offer a diverse range of international job opportunities in various fields.

The Dutch job market has seen a high demand for engineering, health and public services, financial services, IT, project management, research, hospitality, construction, education, and science and research professionals. These sectors have the most open vacancies, making it easier for expats to find employment in their areas of expertise. With a high standard of living, excellent work-life balance, and a welcoming environment for international workers, the Netherlands is an attractive option for those looking to advance their careers and experience a new culture.

Here are some of the sectors with the most job demands:

- engineering
- health and public service
- financial services
- IT
- project management
- research
- hospitality

- construction
- education
- science & research

Chapter 12:

Study Abroad Checklist for Sweden

People are attracted to Sweden for its natural beauty and other exotic factors. However, the students are attracted to Sweden for higher education. One of the reasons students enroll in Swedish Universities is that the average tuition fee for a master's program is approximately USD 14,500 per year; therefore, bachelor's programs are cheaper. The cost of living for students is around USD 900 per month, although this can vary based on location a k part-time while studying, with assistance from consultancies, to find suitable employment.

Students can apply to extend their residence permit upon completing their studies, providing them at least six months to search for employment in Sweden. Many degree programs in the country incorporate internships, providing valuable real-world experience and networking opportunities.

Sweden is home to several multinational corporations, including renowned companies such as IKEA, TetraPak, Volvo, Ericsson, AstraZeneca, Securitas, Spotify, and H&M. Therefore, securing an internship or full-time position with these companies is highly desirable for many students.

Top Ten Universities in Sweden

1. Karolinska Institute

Located in Solna, Stockholm County, the Karolinska Institute, also known as the Royal Caroline Institute, is a renowned medical university focusing on research and education. It has approximately 6,000 students and is located close to the Karolinska University Hospital.

2. Lund University

Established in 1666, Lund University (LU) is a public research university that consistently ranks among the world's top institutions. It is situated in Lund in the province of Scania—a city in southern Sweden near Denmark and Germany. With over 41,000 officially registered students across multiple campuses, LU is one of the Nordic region's largest educational and research institutions.

3. Uppsala University

Founded in 1477, Uppsala University is the oldest university in Sweden and Scandinavia. It is highly regarded for its research and comprises nine faculties distributed over three domains: Humanities and Social Sciences, Medicine and Pharmacy, and Science and Technology. The university hosts more than 52,000 students and roughly 2,200 doctoral students, along with a significant international student population of 12%.

4. KTH Royal Institute of Technology

As Sweden's largest and oldest technical university, KTH Royal Institute of Technology is a leading institution in natural sciences, engineering, architecture, industrial management, and urban planning. It plays a significant role in technical research and education in the country.

5. Stockholm University

Founded in 1878, Stockholm University is one of Scandinavia's oldest and largest universities. It offers diverse subjects and continues the tradition of providing public mathematics, physics, chemistry, and geology lectures.

6. Linkoping University

Ranked at #330 among the Best Global Universities, Linkoping University is known for its exceptional education and research across various disciplines.

7. Chalmers University of Technology

The Chalmers University of Technology holds the #337 spot among the Best Global Universities. It is known for its high performance in various areas, as determined by widely accepted indicators of excellence.

8. Swedish University of Agricultural Sciences

Ranked at #356 among the Best Global Universities, the Swedish University of Agricultural Sciences excels in agricultural sciences based on widely accepted indicators of excellence.

9. Umea University

On the list of Best Global Universities, Umea University ranked 366. It is a well-recognized institution because of how well it performs on several excellence indices.

10. University of Gothenburg

The University of Gothenburg is a public institution whose history goes back to 1891. The Gothenburg University was established in 1954 in Gothenburg, one of Sweden's largest cities, and it offers various facilities throughout the city.

Entry Requirements

The admission criteria for undergraduate programs at Swedish universities are straightforward. Students need to have a high school diploma with a minimum of 60% marks and be at least 18 years old to enroll in a bachelor's degree program.

A demonstration of English proficiency is required, which can be fulfilled by completing English courses equivalent to Swedish upper secondary English Course 6. Additionally, students must have completed mathematics courses at a level comparable to those taught at Swedish universities, typically involving approximately 10 years of mathematics study.

For admission to a master's degree program at a Swedish university, applicants must hold a bachelor's degree from an internationally recognized university or an equivalent qualification to the Swedish *Kandidatexamen*. English proficiency is also necessary, and applicants should aim for a good score on the IELTS or TOEFL exams.

Finding the Right Program

Conduct thorough research to determine the courses and universities that interest you in Sweden. Utilize online resources to explore the various approaches and universities available in the country. Visit the official websites of the universities to gather more information about their programs and courses. Take into consideration your preferred university, desired program, and the location that suits you best. Familiarize yourself with the admission requirements for the specific course and university you intend to apply to.

Scholarships and Funding

Swedish Institute Scholarships for Global Professionals

The Swedish Institute (SI) provides 300 scholarships to international master's students at Swedish higher education institutions. The scholarship covers the entire tuition fees, monthly living expenses of SEK 10,000, health insurance, and airfare of SEK 15,000.

Visby Program:

International master's students from specific nations are given the Visby Program Scholarship. It provides a complete tuition fee waiver,

9,000 SEK in living expenses of SEK 9,000, health insurance, and 5,000 SEK in flights.

Lund University Global Scholarship Program

This merit-based scholarship program grants partial or full tuition fee waivers to exceptional students from non-EU and non-EEA countries studying at Lund University.

The Jönköping University Scholarship

Jönköping University offers scholarships to outstanding students with exceptional academic performance in their bachelor's or master's degree programs. The scholarship covers 30% of the tuition fees.

Halmstad University Scholarships

Halmstad University provides scholarships to international students outside the EU, EEA, and Switzerland. The scholarship amounts to a 25% or 50% tuition fee waiver.

BTH Scholarship

The Blekinge Institute of Technology awards international students a 50% tuition fee reduction scholarship. The university is renowned globally for its software engineering and sustainable development expertise.

Chalmers University Avancez Scholarships

The Chalmers University of Technology, a top Swedish university, offers merit-based scholarships to non-EU international students. The scholarships provide a 75% tuition fee reduction for two-year programs, with additional reductions available for outstanding students.

Dalarna University Scholarship

Dalarna University offers scholarships ranging from 10% to 50% tuition fee reductions, depending on the award. The university is known for its innovative teaching methods and incorporation of technology in education.

GIH Scholarship

The Swedish School of Sport and Health Sciences, GIH, offers full tuition fee waivers for undergraduate and postgraduate courses in sports and health.

Karlstad University Global Scholarship

Karlstad University provides a Global Scholarship Program for academically exceptional students from countries outside Switzerland, the European Union, and the European Economic Area. The scholarship offers reductions of 25%, 50%, 75%, or 100% on tuition fees.

Documentation

The application form is crucial in seeking admission to your chosen university. You must carefully complete the form, online or offline, depending on the availability of application options. Some universities provide an online application process, while others offer paper application forms on their websites.

To gain admission to Swedish universities, you are required to take English language tests to demonstrate your proficiency. These test scores help universities evaluate your abilities and skills necessary for completing the course. Popular English language tests such as TOEFL, IELTS, or PTE are accepted for master's or business programs.

Along with the application form, you must submit academic certificates as evidence of your educational qualifications. If you have recently completed your higher secondary studies and are applying for undergraduate studies, you must provide your SSC and higher secondary certificates. For applicants with a completed bachelor's or master's degree, degree certificates and mark sheets should be included. Academic credentials encompass various documents such as SSC, intermediate, bachelor's degree, master's degree, and relevant project work details.

The Statement of Purpose (SOP) is a concise essay highlighting your career goals, research objectives, and achievements thus far. In the SOP, you should explain why you have chosen the course, your reasons for selecting a particular university, your post-course plans, and your personal interests. A well-crafted SOP is pivotal in securing admission, so allocate ample time to prepare it before submission.

A Letter of Recommendation is a requested letter written by someone who can assess your qualities, characteristics, and capabilities to perform a specific task. Universities typically require recommendation letters to gain insights into an applicant's suitability. It is crucial to find the right person who can provide a strong recommendation letter to enhance your chances of admission.

Applicants applying to Business Programs often require relevant work experience to secure admission to a Business School in Sweden. However, undergraduate applicants do not typically need prior work experience. The idocuments to support work experience include joining letters, salary slips, and employment certificates from previous employers.

In addition to the above documents, a well-prepared resume detailing your educational background and skill set is required. Creating a powerful resume is advisable, and seeking assistance to craft an impactful one is prudent.

Although seemingly simple, providing correctly sized and up-to-date photographs with your application is essential. Failure to attach the appropriate photographs may result in the rejection of your application.

If you have additional documents showcasing your paper presentations, organizational skills in symposiums, or other relevant achievements, you can include them alongside the required documents. These certificates can further strengthen your application and highlight your talents and extracurricular activities.

Upon receiving your application, the university will verify your documents and profile before issuing an offer letter. If you do not meet any of the university's requirements, or if there are doubts about the authenticity of the student, the administration can reject the application. Once you receive the offer letter, you can apply for a student visa by submitting the necessary documents.

PR / Citizenship

The most convenient and efficient way to apply for a residence permit to study at universities and colleges in Sweden is through online application. Online applications are given priority and directly sent to the Swedish Migration Agency. It is essential to have your permit granted before entering Sweden, regardless of the application method chosen.

To be eligible for a permanent residence permit, you must hold a research residence permit for at least four years within seven years. If necessary, time spent with a work or doctoral studies permit can also count towards this requirement.

To qualify for a permanent residence permit, you must:

- Meet the requirements for a continued residence permit.
- Have resided in Sweden with a valid residence permit for a specific period of time.
- Demonstrate the ability to support yourself financially.
- Maintain a law-abiding lifestyle.

The first two requirements may vary depending on the type of permit you currently hold, while the last two requirements apply universally to anyone seeking a permanent residence permit. Therefore, it is necessary to consider this information in conjunction with the requirements for obtaining an extended residence permit.

Different rules apply for permanent residence permits for individuals with a residence permit for upper secondary level studies or a license intended to facilitate job search after completing studies at the upper secondary level.

Job Opportunities

Sweden is renowned for offering some of the most exceptional benefits in the world, encompassing healthcare, education, and generous vacation allowances. As a result, the country boasts promising job opportunities, making it an appealing destination for individuals seeking high living standards and social welfare. Despite Sweden's high tax rates, the prospect of pursuing a lucrative career abroad in this nation remains enticing. With competitive salaries, excellent perks, and a growing array of possibilities, Sweden has garnered a formidable reputation for its workforce. The country has diligently built robust and efficient institutions that offer employees long-term prospects, reflecting the collective efforts of its people.

High-demand jobs in Sweden:

- Surgeons/Doctors
- Engineers
- Sales and purchasing
- Marketing director
- Finance and Administration
- Software and System Developers
- Teachers
- Pilots
- Lawyer
- Orthodontist

Chapter 13:
Study Abroad Checklist for Switzerland

Switzerland, a small European nation, warmly welcomes students from around the world, making it an attractive destination for international education. Renowned for its exceptional universities, groundbreaking research centers, and investment in cutting-edge industries, Switzerland offers ample opportunities. Students living in Zurich and Geneva can access art galleries, museums, theaters, and live music venues. Furthermore, Switzerland's proximity to iconic natural wonders, including the magnificent Alps, allows students to explore breathtaking mountain valleys and peaks within a few hours.

Switzerland's major cities, serving as global hubs for finance, technology, and innovation, exude a cosmopolitan atmosphere due to their diverse population drawn from across the globe. The country boasts four official languages: German, French, Italian, and Romansh. Moreover, each language exhibits regional variations throughout Switzerland's 26 regions. English is also widely spoken, particularly in businesses, universities, and cities such as Zurich, Geneva, and Bern.

While university degrees are predominantly taught in French and German, many Swiss universities offer programs in English. These institutions attract international students, creating vibrant and dynamic campuses that serve as melting pots of various cultures. For example, the University of Geneva, with its student body of around 16,000, proudly hosts approximately 40% international students.

Top 10 Universities In Switzerland

ETH Zurich - Swiss Federal Institute of Technology

At ETH Zurich, students are immersed in an environment that fosters independent thinking, while researchers are motivated by a climate that encourages outstanding performance. Located in the heart of Europe, ETH Zurich forges connections worldwide and pioneers effective solutions to current and future global challenges.

Swiss Federal Institute of Technology in Lausanne (EPFL)

Switzerland has consistently maintained its global leadership in research and education, and EPFL epitomizes the country's commitment to innovation. EPFL's researchers continually achieve remarkable results and distinctions, while homegrown entrepreneurs contribute to its vibrant ecosystem. The institute also establishes international networks with other centers of excellence.

University of Applied Sciences and Arts Western Switzerland (HES-SO)

Playing a significant role in the socio-economic and cultural development of the seven cantons of Western Switzerland, HES-SO comprises six faculties and a network of schools of higher education. It is widely recognized within Switzerland and internationally as a key player in higher education.

University of Basel

Renowned for its outstanding achievements in research and teaching, the University of Basel holds an esteemed international reputation. Founded in 1460, it is Switzerland's oldest university, boasting a rich history of success spanning over 550 years.

University of Bern

Although offering top-quality education across a wide range of disciplines, the University of Bern is regarded highly for its excellence in teaching and research. It provides a delightful academic setting and a campus intimately connected to the city's social, economic, and political fabric.

University of Fribourg

A hub of simultaneous learning, research, employment, and events, the University of Fribourg holds significant influence in the commercial and cultural life of the region. Its innovative spirit drives its engagement in various domains.

University of Geneva

Founded by Jean Calvin in 1559, the University of Geneva is committed to fostering critical thinking, teaching, dialogue, and research. With a diverse student body of over 16,500 individuals from over 150 countries, UNIGE offers a broad range of programs, including bachelor's and master's degrees, doctoral programs, and continuing education courses across numerous fields.

University of Lausanne

The University of Lausanne (UNIL) offers an international atmosphere, with one-fifth of its student population and one-third of its teaching staff from abroad.

University of Neuchâtel

At the University of Neuchâtel (UniNE), professors must meet high pedagogical standards to share their knowledge with students in an inspiring manner effectively.

University of St. Gallen (HSG)

With a history spanning over a century, the University of St. Gallen (HSG) has evolved from a "business academy" to a distinguished university. HSG provides students with a valuable blend of research and practical experience. A commitment to excellence in teaching and research is deeply ingrained in the university's culture, ensuring a conducive environment for exceptional achievements.

Entry Requirements

Applying to study at a Swiss university is a straightforward process, but applicants should keep some essential advice in mind before submitting their applications. Here are the key points to remember:

Explore Study Options: Switzerland offers diverse study programs, many of which strongly focus on research. It is essential to gather information about your chosen discipline before deciding.

Review Study Programs: Take the time to carefully examine all the study programs offered by different universities and degree levels to ensure they align with your academic goals and interests.

Check Entry Requirements: Thoroughly understand the entry requirements for each study degree or program you are interested in. Specific admission criteria are set for medicine, dentistry, and veterinary degrees.

Seek Scholarships: Look for available scholarships for international students in Switzerland. Scholarships can provide financial support and make studying in Switzerland more accessible.

How to Apply for University Studies in Switzerland:

- **Complete Online Application**: Fill out the application form online, typically available on the university's website.
- **Pay Application Fees:** Ensure you submit the required application fees within the specified timeframe.
- **Submit Supporting Documents:** Upload all the necessary documents that support your application before the deadline. These documents may include academic transcripts, language proficiency certificates, CVs, motivation letters, identification copies, and passport photos.

Language Requirements:

Official Teaching Languages: Switzerland has three official teaching languages: German, French, and Italian. The university determines the language of instruction, but many universities offer a wide range of English, German, and French study programs.

Language Proficiency Tests: Accepted evidence of language proficiency includes tests such as DSH, TestDaF, OSD, telc (for German), DELF, DALF (for French), and IELTS or TOEFL (for English). If you do not have a language proficiency certificate, some universities offer language tests to assess your level.

Swiss Universities Admission Requirements:

Prepare Required Documents: Gather necessary documents, including a printed copy of the application form, passport photos, ID copies, academic transcripts, high school or bachelor's diploma, language proficiency certificate, CV, evidence of application fee payment, and a personal essay or motivation letter.

Submitting the Application: Since Swiss universities do not have a centralized admission system, you must visit each university's website and follow their specific requirements and procedures. Most universities have an admission portal for direct application submission.

Doctoral Program Applications: If applying for a doctoral program, you may need a letter from a certified supervisor who agrees to supervise your research. Additionally, your certificates and transcripts may need to be translated into French, English, German, or Italian. Some universities may also require an official document explaining your previous university's grading and assessment system.

By following these guidelines, you can ensure a smooth and successful application process for studying at a Swiss university.

Finding the Right Program

Selecting the right path of study, institution, and location requires ample time and careful consideration. It is crucial to initiate the search process early and make well-informed decisions. Follow these phases to navigate the journey successfully:

Phase 1: Researching and Deciding

Identify your needs and preferences. Evaluate the profiles of institutions and courses that align with your interests, eliminating those that don't meet your criteria.

Compile a list of 10-15 institutions to gather more detailed information. Review the information received and request additional details before finalizing your selection.

Phase 2: Applying

Begin by completing the application process meticulously, ensuring you don't overlook any important aspects. Consult the respective institutions for the required documents.

Some courses and institutions may require an interview, so prepare adequately.

Apply to accredited institutions and verify if they meet the minimum standards. Explore their official websites for more information on accreditation.

Admission Requirements at Different Levels of Study

For Bachelor's Studies:

The primary admission requirement for Bachelor's programs is a Swiss secondary high-school leaving certificate called *Matura*. Alternatively, a foreign secondary high-school leaving certificate deemed equivalent may also be accepted.

Students without a recognized certificate may need to undergo a university entrance exam.

By following these steps and being mindful of the admission requirements, you can effectively navigate the application process and increase your chances of gaining admission to your desired program and institution.

Scholarships

Swiss Excellence Scholarships for Foreign Scholars and Artists

The Swiss Government presents scholarships annually to foster international exchange and research collaboration between Switzerland and more than 180 other countries. These Swiss Government Excellence Scholarships are designed for young researchers from abroad who have completed a master's or PhD's and foreign artists with a bachelor's degree.

ETH Zurich Excellence Scholarships in Switzerland

ETH Zurich, ranked seventh globally, is Switzerland's premier university and the only non-European institution in the top ten. The ETH Zurich Excellence Scholarships support students pursuing master's studies in Switzerland by providing scholarships, mentorship, and a network facilitated by the ETH Foundation. These scholarships cover the entire academic program and living costs during the master's program. The ETH-D Scholarship includes a partial stipend and additional opportunities such as assistantships or extra scholarships provided by the department.

University of Zurich Scholarships for International Students

As the largest university in Switzerland, with approximately 25,500 students, the University of Zurich offers a wide range of academic options. It holds second in national rankings among all Swiss universities and is currently ranked 78th worldwide. The University of Zurich conducts extensive teaching and research across diverse fields, surpassing the scope of ETH Zurich and the specialized EPFL. Its facilities are spread throughout the vicinity of Zurich.

University of Bern International Scholarships

The University of Bern is renowned for its commitment to delivering high-quality education and research services. Recognized for its excellent teaching standards, it provides a stimulating environment and maintains strong ties to campus life's social, economic, and political aspects.

Ecole Polytechnique Fédérale de Lausanne Scholarships

The Ecole Polytechnique Fédérale de Lausanne (EPFL) offers numerous scholarship opportunities for international students, including scholarships for bachelor's, master's, and doctoral programs. EPFL is committed to providing a conducive environment for students pursuing their academic aspirations.

University of Basel International Scholarships

The University of Basel offers scholarships through its Senate Scholarship Committee in addition to any education contributions provided by the canton. International students are encouraged to explore the available scholarship options for which they are eligible. Situated in the vibrant city of Basel, the University of Basel thrives on innovation and draws inspiration from its rich artistic heritage.

University of Lausanne Scholarships

The University of Lausanne provides several scholarships for students interested in studying at the institution, including merit-based scholarships, Swiss Government Scholarships, and World Bank Scholarships. The University of Lausanne has seven faculties dedicated to delivering quality education and research. It hosts approximately 15,600 students and employs around 3,900 research, teaching, and technical staff.

University of Geneva Scholarships

The University of Geneva prioritizes teaching, research, and community service. With over 17,000 students representing 150 diverse nationalities, it is the second-largest university in Switzerland. The university actively promotes excellence in education and research.

University of Lausanne Master's Grants for Foreign Students

The University of Lausanne offers scholarships to international students pursuing a master's degree through the UNIL Master's

Grants. These grants provide a monthly amount of CHF (Swiss Frank) 1600 from September 15th to July 15th for a duration not exceeding the minimum prescribed period of the program.

Geneva Academy of International Humanitarian Law and Human Rights Scholarships

The Geneva Academy provides partial and full scholarships for its Master of Laws (LLM) in International Humanitarian Law and Human Rights and Master of Advanced Studies in Transitional Justice, Human Rights, and the Rule of Law (MTJ). Full scholarships cover tuition and living expenses in Geneva for ten months, while partial scholarships cover tuition fees.

Considering these scholarship opportunities, students and artists can benefit from financial support while pursuing their academic and artistic aspirations in Switzerland.

PR / Citizenship

You must fulfill specific requirements to become eligible for Swiss citizenship through naturalization. These include residing in Switzerland for a minimum of 10 years, possessing a valid residence permit, demonstrating proficiency in one of Switzerland's official languages, and showcasing a strong integration into Swiss society.

For permanent residence in Switzerland, the primary requirement is the duration of one's stay in the country with a valid residence permit, typically a "B" or "L" permit. The standard residency requirement is 10 years. However, certain individuals, such as EU/EFTA citizens, American and Canadian citizens, and spouses and children aged 12-18 of Swiss citizens or "C" permit holders, may be eligible to apply after five years.

Specific requirements and procedures for obtaining a "C" permit may vary among Swiss cantons. Therefore, it is necessary to contact the local cantonal immigration office to obtain accurate information on the following steps.

Generally, the application process involves completing an application form and providing the following documents:

- Valid identification
- Proof of address in Switzerland
- Evidence of an existing residence permit (e.g., "B" or "L" permit)
- Verification of meeting the requirements, such as language certificates

Switzerland issues biometric permanent residence permits in the form of a credit card design. These permits incorporate a microchip that stores the holder's biometric data and allows visa-free travel within the Schengen area.

Job Opportunities

Switzerland has become a sought-after destination for expatriates in search of employment opportunities. While finding a job can be challenging, Switzerland offers some of Europe's highest minimum wages and average salaries. However, it is essential to note that the Swiss work culture expects high dedication and effort. Here are a few of the highest-paying professions in Switzerland:

IT Systems Architect

IT system architecture ranks among the most lucrative professions in Switzerland. Systems architects are vital in designing, configuring, operating, and maintaining computer and networking systems for businesses and organizations, ensuring smooth and efficient operations.

Judge

Becoming a judge requires a strong educational background and specific skills. Typically, judges hold a law degree and gain experience as lawyers. Passing a competitive exam is also a requirement for federal administrative law judges.

Chief Executive Officer (CEO)

Chief executive officer positions often necessitate a combination of education and training, such as a bachelor's degree and extensive business and industry experience. CEOs hold crucial leadership roles within organizations.

Chief Financial Officer (CFO)

CFOs are responsible for managing a company's financial affairs. To become a CFO, individuals usually need a bachelor's degree and experience in a business or economic occupation.

Physician

Physicians play a crucial role in providing quality healthcare to patients. They typically hold a bachelor's degree followed by a medical degree from a medical school, which usually takes four more years to complete. Physicians may also need to complete an internship, depending on their chosen specialty.

It's important to note that these professions require varying education, training, and experience. Pursuing these careers in Switzerland can offer significant financial rewards, but it's crucial to meet the qualifications and dedicate oneself to professional excellence.

Chapter 14:

Study Abroad Checklist for the Russian Federation

According to information from the Organization for Economic Cooperation and Development (OECD), the Russian Federation (formerly known as the USSR, "Russia") claims to be one of the most highly educated populations globally, surpassing Canada, Japan, Israel, and the USA. Over half of the Russian populace holds higher education qualifications. Additionally, Russia attracts more than 200,000 international students and individuals from 168 countries enrolling in the Russian Federation universities.

Higher education in the Russian Federation is known for its excellence, earning a reputation comparable to the "Made in Russia" seal of quality in other industries. Russia's long-standing university tradition is especially recognized in fields like engineering and science. Graduating from a Russian university is highly regarded by employers worldwide.

Russia's higher education system offers a wide array of options to cater to diverse interests. With almost 450 state-accredited universities and approximately 17,500 degree programs, students can pursue studies in nearly every subject and academic level, ranging from bachelor's to doctoral degrees. Furthermore, an increasing number of courses and degree programs are now offered in English to accommodate international students, making it accessible to those who may not be fluent in Russian yet.

Embracing cultural diversity, around twelve percent of students in Russian universities are from foreign countries, providing an excellent opportunity for students like yourself to connect with people from various parts of the world, gain exposure to different cultures, and broaden their horizons.

Top 10 Universities

Lomonosov Moscow State University (MSU):

Lomonosov Moscow State University (MSU) is a prominent public research university in Moscow. The institution encompasses 15 research institutes, 43 faculties, over 300 departments, and six branches.

Novosibirsk State University:

Novosibirsk State University is a well-established public research university in Novosibirsk, Russia. It was founded in 1958 and is dedicated to integrating education and science, involving students in research activities from an early stage, and engaging leading scientists in its teaching programs.

Tomsk State University:

The National Research Tomsk State University (TSU) is a distinguished public research university in Tomsk, Russia. It was established in 1888; it is the first university in the Asian part of Russia and the pioneering Russian university East of the Volga.

Moscow Institute of Physics and Technology (MIPT):

Moscow Institute of Physics and Technology is a renowned public research university in Moscow Oblast, Russia. It specializes in producing theoretical and applied physics experts, applied mathematics, and related disciplines.

St Petersburg University:

Saint Petersburg State University is a prestigious public research university in Saint Petersburg, Russia. Founded in 1724 by a decree of Peter the Great, the university has always focused on fundamental research in science, engineering, and humanities.

Peoples' Friendship University of Russia:

The Patrice Lumumba Peoples' Friendship University of Russia, also known as RUDN University and previously known as Patrice Lumumba University, is a distinguished public research university in Moscow, Russia. It holds the name of the Congolese politician Patrice Lumumba.

Higher School of Economics (HSE):

HSE University, officially the National Research University Higher School of Economics, is a reputable public research university founded in 1992 and headquartered in Moscow, Russia.

National Research Nuclear University MEPhI (Moscow Engineering Physics Institute):

National Research Nuclear University MEPhI is a technical university in Russia. Constructed in 1942 as the Moscow Mechanical Institute of Munitions, it was later renamed the Moscow Mechanical Institute.

Sechenov First Moscow State Medical University:

First, Moscow State Medical University (MSMU) is the oldest medical university in Russia, located in Moscow. It has received notable rankings from various international organizations.

Peter the Great St. Petersburg Polytechnic University:

Peter, the Great St. Petersburg Polytechnic University, also known as SPbPU, is a distinguished technical university in Saint Petersburg,

Russia. It has undergone name changes, previously known as Peter the Great Polytechnic Institute and Kalinin Polytechnic Institute.

Entry Requirements

The admission requirements for international students in Russia are relatively lenient, given that the applicants follow the necessary procedures. Russia welcomes foreign citizens with educational qualifications equivalent to the level of general secondary education as required. All required documents must be translated into the Russian language. Once the candidate receives an official invitation from Russia, they must present it to the Russian Embassy to obtain a visa.

International students are granted admission to universities in Russia after undergoing a mandatory medical examination (which is compensated) in a medical facility at their place of study. This examination aims to confirm that they have no health-related obstacles to studying in Russia. The cost of the initial medical examination is approximately 58 USD.

Health services for accepted international students are available on a compensation basis. Moreover, students must have a contract for compulsory medical insurance, typically costing around 85 EUR per year. This insurance ensures that they receive medical assistance in case of emergencies. Additionally, foreign students must undergo an annual medical examination, which costs approximately 35 USD annually.

Finding the Right Program

Russia has gained international recognition for its excellent education system and wide range of academic disciplines. It is advisable to start researching and preparing several months in advance to secure a place in the right program.

Begin by identifying your area of interest and conducting thorough research on the courses or subjects you wish to pursue. Visit the official websites of universities, institutes, or colleges to gather information about admission requirements, available courses, and important dates and deadlines. Create a list of potential educational institutions that offer programs aligned with your interests and check if you meet their admission criteria.

Consider visiting the campuses of the shortlisted educational institutions. This will allow you to learn more about the courses and the institutions themselves. Engage in discussions with faculty members and students to seek answers to any questions.

After meticulous research and campus visits, make a well-informed final decision. While choosing, consider factors such as affordability, proximity to your location, financial considerations, the level of engagement and involvement in the program, and most importantly, how well the chosen course aligns with your academic and career goals.

Once you decide on the course and educational institution, ensure that you submit your application on time. Check with the respective university or institute for specific admission requirements and the necessary documents to include with your application. Planning and preparing well in advance will increase your chances of a successful application and entry into the program of your choice.

Scholarships

Berklee on the Road Clinics:

These clinics offer educational sessions conducted by Berklee College of Music to students interested in pursuing music as a career. The program aims to enrich students' musical knowledge and skills through interactive workshops.

Drs. Anthony and Joanne Edmonds Study Abroad Scholarship:

This scholarship, awarded biennially, provides financial assistance to a Department of History student who plans to study abroad. The award alternates between the Department of History and the Honors College.

Spreadsheet Gladiator Scholarship:

Coefficient offers an annual scholarship worth USD 1,500 to college students pursuing Business, Computer Science, or Communications degrees. The scholarship recognizes individuals who utilize spreadsheets extensively in their day-to-day tasks and careers.

Pinsky Law New Venture Development Scholarship:

Pinsky Law supports entrepreneurs and startup companies, providing legal resources for startups on their websites. They offer this scholarship to assist students interested in business ventures, recognizing the financial challenges of establishing and operating new ventures.

Anonymous Hope Fund:

This fund supports personal proposals, with approximately 93% of the legitimate submissions receiving funding annually, totaling over 670,000 proposals annually.

Fighting Bullying With Technology:

This scholarship program aims to support students who have experienced bullying financially, actively fought against bullying, or are working to make their schools and communities safer, tolerant, and diverse using technology.

Erasmus Mundus Joint Masters Scholarships:

The European Union supports jointly recognized Master's degrees to promote excellence and internationalization among participating institutions.

Education Future International Scholarship:

Scholarship winners worldwide have contributed to creating this unique scholarship fund, intending to support the next generation of students pursuing education financially.

F.L. McEwen Scholarship:

Established in recognition of F.L. McEwen's contributions as Dean of OAC (1983-90), this scholarship prioritizes students with research interests in sustainable agriculture and involvement in related extracurricular activities.

Ethel Rose Charney Scholarship in the Human/Animal Bond:

This scholarship is initially offered as an entrance award, with the potential to be held by master's and doctoral students up to three times and two times, respectively. Students must apply annually for consideration. The scholarship aims to support research related to the human-animal bond.

Documents Required

After receiving an acceptance upon the conclusion of their invitation, international students must prepare the required documents upon arriving in Russia. The necessary documents include:

- Educational Certificate should include a comprehensive list of all studied subjects and corresponding marks.
- Medical Certificate: Obtained from an official public health service in the student's home country.
- AIDS Test Certificate: Issued by an official public health service in the country where the student is arriving from.
- Copy of Birth Notification.
- 10 passport-sized photos (4 x 6 cm).
- National Passport with Russian Study Visa.
- Notarized Translations: All documents must be translated into Russian and notarized.

The application vetting process is completed once all the required documents have been submitted. Successful students are usually notified of their acceptance within 2-3 weeks, and a formal acceptance letter is issued upon payment of the tuition down payment. Afterward, students can proceed with registration, enroll in their chosen study program, and select courses for the desired start semester.

Citizenship / PR

To become a Russian citizen, individuals must meet specific criteria, which include being born on Russian soil to Russian citizens or permanent resident parents or living continuously in Russia with a temporary residency permit for at least five years.

Foreign nationals interested in obtaining Russian nationality can apply after residing in Russia for at least five years with a permanent residence permit. Acquiring a permanent residence permit is the initial step towards Russian citizenship and offers numerous benefits similar to those that Russian citizens enjoy.

The Russian permanent residence permit is valid for five years and can be renewed as required. The Russian General Directorate of Migratory Affairs issues it.

Russian citizenship can be obtained through naturalization for foreign citizens or by birth if one's parents have Russian origins.

While many individuals may opt for a permanent residence permit, obtaining Russian citizenship offers additional advantages. These include the ability to establish a business or work as a sole trader, full access to social services in Russia, and the privilege of traveling to and from Russia without needing a visa.

Job Opportunities

Being aware of the earning potential in various career opportunities in Russia can be advantageous, especially for young individuals seeking highly paid sectors. Here is a list of some of the highest-paying jobs in Russia, along with their corresponding salary scales:

- Ship Captain — 500,000 RUB
- Aircraft Commander — 320,000 RUB
- Chief Technologist in the gold mining industry — 312,000 RUB
- Head Coach of the ice hockey team — 300,000 RUB

- Construction Site Manager — 250,000 RUB
- Dentist — 200,000 RUB
- Risk Manager — 200,000 RUB
- Electrical Engineer — 195,000 RUB
- IT Analyst — 190,000 RUB
- Aircraft Co-pilot — 180,000 RUB

While securing a well-paying job in Russia can be challenging, especially for foreigners seeking better opportunities, it is not impossible. Many individuals are employed daily, and the possibilities for lucrative careers remain positive.

Various channels can be explored to conduct job research, including online recruitment platforms, LinkedIn, or by directly submitting your CV and cover letter to companies. Staying persistent and proactive in the job search can increase your chances of landing a high-paying job offer in Russia.

Chapter 15:
Study Abroad Checklist for India

India, renowned for its rich cultural diversity and being the birthplace of several major world religions, presents many enticing options for international students seeking educational opportunities abroad. While contemplating the idea of studying in one of the most captivating countries in the world may appear daunting initially, it can ultimately lead to unparalleled perspectives and experiences. Studying in India offers a fresh outlook and a rewarding and affordable experience despite international students' potential challenges while adapting to life here.

India's allure lies in its vibrant traditions, bustling cities, and rapidly growing economy. With an extensive education system, the country boasts numerous top-ranking universities, making it an appealing destination for international students. A testament to this is India's impressive performance in the 2023 QS ranking of world universities, where 41 Indian universities secured positions among the 1422 universities listed. Furthermore, the fact that seven of these entries were new additions demonstrates India's educational institutions' continuous growth and development.

Considering all India offers, one might wonder, "Why not study in India?" This diverse nation promises a wealth of learning and personal growth opportunities, making it an excellent choice for international students seeking a transformative educational experience.

Top 10 Universities

Indian Institute of Science, Bangalore:

The Indian Institute of Science in Bangalore is a government-recognized research university dedicated to higher education and research in science, engineering, design, and management.

Indian Institute of Technology, Bombay:

Located in Powai, Mumbai, Maharashtra, India, the Indian Institute of Technology Bombay is a renowned public research university and technical institute. It is the topmost preferred choice for Indian students pursuing STEM fields like computer science and engineering.

Indian Institute of Technology, Kharagpur:

The Indian Institute of Technology Kharagpur, established by the Government of India in Kharagpur, West Bengal, is a public institute of technology and research university. It is the first of the IITs and is recognized as an Institute of National Importance.

Indian Institute of Technology, Madras:

Situated in Chennai, Tamil Nadu, India, the Indian Institute of Technology Madras is a distinguished public technical university. It has been selected as one of India's eight public Institutes of Eminence.

Indian Institute of Technology, Delhi:

Among the Twenty-Three IITs designed as Centers of Excellence for training, research, and development in science, engineering, and technology, the Indian Institute of Technology Delhi is prominent in India.

University of Delhi:

Formally known as the University of Delhi, this central university in Delhi, India, was founded in 1922. It holds the status of an Institute of Eminence, as recognized by the University Grants Commission.

All India Institute of Medical Sciences, New Delhi:

The All India Institute of Medical Sciences, AIIMS Delhi, is a public medical research university and hospital in New Delhi, India. It operates autonomously under the Ministry of Health and Family Welfare, following the AIIMS Act 1956.

Indian Institute of Technology, Kanpur:

The Indian Institute of Technology Kanpur, situated in Kanpur, Uttar Pradesh, India, is a notable public institute of technology. It was declared an Institute of National Importance by the Government of India under the Institutes of Technology Act.

Jadavpur University, Kolkata:

Jadavpur University, a public state university in Jadavpur, Kolkata, West Bengal, India, was initially established as Bengal Technical Institute in 1905. It later transformed into Jadavpur University in 1955 and, in 2023, ranked fourth among Indian universities according to the National Institutional Ranking Framework.

Jawaharlal Nehru University:

Jawaharlal Nehru University (JNU), a major public research university in New Delhi, India, was founded in 1969 and named after India's first Prime Minister, Jawaharlal Nehru. It is renowned for its leading faculties and research focus on social sciences and applied sciences.

Entry Requirements

All international students, excluding those from the United Kingdom, must fulfill our English language requirements. If you do not meet the required score, you may be eligible to enroll in our pre-sessional English language course.

Standard XII scores will not be considered for meeting our English Language requirements. Instead, applicants must complete an approved English Language test.

For Undergraduate programs:

- A minimum of 70% in Standard XII Higher Secondary School Certificate for CBSE, CISCE, Tamil Nadu, Maharashtra, and West Bengal boards.
- A minimum of 80% in Standard XII Higher Secondary School Certificate for other state boards.
- For Postgraduate taught courses in ECE (Electronic and Computer Engineering):
- Bachelor's degree with a minimum CGPA of 6.5 out of 10 (equivalent to 2:2).
- For Postgraduate taught courses in all other fields:
- Bachelor's degree with a minimum CGPA of 6.0 out of 10 (equivalent to 2:2).

Work experience may be required for certain courses. Specific course entry details can be found in the postgraduate prospectus.

Finding the Right Course

Every course is a unique blend of various elements, encompassing subjects covered, campus location, and potential career paths. Whether you are still considering different programs, weighing options between two fields of study, or unsure about your career aspirations, we are here to assist you in finding the most suitable course and coordinating your university application.

Start by jotting down a list of your interests and skills, and take some time to reflect on them. Identify the ones that show promise for pursuing as a career, and eliminate options that are merely hobbies. Creating a more focused and concise list of potential options will help you determine the best courses for your goals.

To make a well-informed decision and maximize your study abroad experience, utilize our course search feature to explore the available avenues tailored to your preferences.

Once you have narrowed your options, assess the qualifications required to pursue each path. Do you meet all the requirements? If not, consider whether you are willing to wait for another intake to fulfill the prerequisites or contemplate switching your area of focus. This decision may be challenging, but we are here to offer guidance and support.

Documents Required

You must submit certificates and diplomas from a recognized international higher education institution, verifying the completion of your degree(s). These documents must be officially issued by the Academic Registrar's Office, the Examinations Office, or the equivalent authority responsible for issuing official transcripts at your university.

It would be best if you also handed in transcripts of completed courses and grades for each semester within your degree. If you have transferred credits from previous studies, include official course transcripts. These transcripts should also be officially issued by the relevant office at your university.

Lastly, you need evidence that you meet the specific entry requirements for your chosen course or program. It is essential to refer to your university's website for information on the particular entry requirements and any additional documentation they may request, such as dissertations, essay summaries, letters of recommendation, or letters of intent. Only submit other documentation if explicitly requested by the university.

Citizenship / PR

A student visa is issued to those who plan to study in a recognized and approved academic institution in India. This visa applies to professional courses like Engineering, Medicine, Law, Management, etc., conducted by recognized educational institutions.

For school-level studies, a student visa is granted only to attend recognized international schools that admit international students and have higher fees.

Student visas are also available for music, dance, yoga, etc., but only in institutions recognized by the Ministry of Home Affairs, New Delhi.

Regarding permanent residency, there are different registration and naturalization options under the Citizenship Act 1955 for individuals of Indian origin, married to Indian citizens, or born to Indian parents. The Act also covers birth registration at Indian consulates and procedures for renouncing or resuming Indian citizenship.

Job Opportunities

Highest Paying Jobs in India:

Project Management:

Leading the list of highest-paying jobs in India, Project Managers play a crucial role in overseeing projects and ensuring successful execution from start to finish.

Artificial Intelligence (AI) Engineer:

In high demand, AI Engineers develop intelligent software systems that continuously learn and improve, making them an essential part of cutting-edge technological advancements.

Data Scientist:

Regarded as one of the most promising careers by LinkedIn, Data Scientists excel in collecting, analyzing, and interpreting vast amounts of data to drive informed decisions for organizations.

Machine Learning Engineer:

As a subset of AI, Machine Learning holds significant potential and projects remarkable growth, offering lucrative opportunities for skilled professionals.

Blockchain Developer:

Blockchain Technology is revolutionizing various sectors, and Blockchain Developers are sought after to implement secure and efficient solutions for currency transactions, data handling, and more.

Full Stack Software Developer:

Software Developers, particularly Full Stack Software Developers, are highly sought-after due to their expertise in developing both the front-end and back-end of software and websites.

The job market in India offers exciting opportunities in various high-paying fields. Professionals in Project Management hold a prominent position in ensuring successful project execution. Artificial Intelligence Engineers are crucial in advancing cutting-edge technology, while Data Scientists contribute significantly to data-driven decision-making.

Machine Learning Engineers are well-positioned to benefit from the growing AI landscape. Blockchain Developers are revolutionizing industries with secure and efficient solutions. Full Stack Software Developers remain in high demand, showcasing their software and website development versatility.

As India continues to embrace technological advancements, these top-paying careers promise a bright future for skilled and ambitious individuals.

Chapter 16:

Study Abroad Checklist for Germany

Studying in Europe is a coveted aspiration for many students, and Germany stands out as one of the most popular destinations, especially for Indian students seeking education abroad. Renowned for its prestigious universities, Germany offers a dream destination for students with its world-class education, multicultural environment, affordable lifestyle, picturesque landscapes, vibrant nightlife, and delectable cuisine.

In Germany, international universities provide diverse courses, including opportunities for research and skill-based training, allowing students to explore new educational avenues and broaden their horizons. Some programs even allow students to pursue multiple courses simultaneously, enabling them to follow their passions while studying at the university.

An overseas college experience in Germany fosters interactions with individuals not just from Germany but from around the globe, leading to the development of valuable intercultural communication skills. One essential aspect of studying in Germany is learning German since English may not be commonly spoken, particularly outside academic circles. Proficiency in German can significantly enhance job prospects, particularly in fields like international relations and diplomacy, where foreign language expertise is highly valued.

Studying abroad offers students a competitive edge when entering the professional world. It demonstrates to employers qualities like courage, adaptability, cultural awareness, and understanding of different work environments and perspectives. These attributes make international degree holders highly sought after by employers, leading to unmatched job opportunities and attractive pay packages, especially from top tech companies.

Top 10 Universities

Technical University of Munich (TUM)

TUM derives its strength from the excellence in research and education of its seven TUM Schools and fosters transdisciplinary innovations through mission-driven Integrative Research Institutes. Embracing rapid societal changes in the digitalization era, TUM has revolutionized the concept of engineering by integrating natural and life sciences, medicine, business management, humanities, and social sciences.

LMU Munich (Ludwig Maximilian University of Munich)

As one of Europe's foremost research universities with a history spanning 500 years, LMU prides itself on its excellence in teaching and research across diverse fields. From humanities and cultural studies to law, economics, social sciences, medicine, and natural sciences, LMU's academic pursuits are comprehensive and impactful.

Heidelberg University

Heidelberg University offers 36 undergraduate courses, four graduate programs, and 16 minors, offering students various academic options. The university's innovative honors program, "The Life of the Mind," enables students to study thematic areas. With a strong international presence and a long-standing exchange program, Heidelberg fosters global connections and embraces a diverse international student body.

Charité - Universitätsmedizin Berlin

With a remarkable legacy of producing more than half of Germany's Nobel prize winners in medicine and physiology, Charité is a prestigious medical university. Its history spans 300 years, and today, it is a significant employer in Berlin, boasting a turnover of €1.5 billion per annum and housing 3,700 doctors.

Humboldt University of Berlin (HU Berlin)

Recognized as a pioneering higher education institution in Europe, HU Berlin owes its reputation to Wilhelm von Humboldt's model, emphasizing a close relationship between research and teaching—a model widely adopted by universities worldwide.

University of Tübingen (Eberhard Karls University of Tübingen)

As a respected academic authority in humanities, natural sciences, and theology, the University of Tübingen is significant among traditional German university towns. Renowned for its boat trips and the stunning architecture of its old town, Hölderlin.

University of Bonn

Ranked among the world's leading research universities, the University of Bonn is home to a diverse community of over 35,000 students and 4,500 academic staff. With strategic partnerships with 70 universities worldwide, the university fosters a strong international atmosphere, welcoming around 4,000 international students annually.

Free University of Berlin

Hosting a vibrant student body of over 32,000 and offering over 150 degree programs, the Free University of Berlin is a hub of academic excellence. With collaborative research centers, an extensive academic staff, and international partnerships, the university maintains a global outlook through its liaison offices in major cities worldwide.

RWTH Aachen University

Renowned for its strong ties with industry, RWTH Aachen has developed a European equivalent of Silicon Valley around its campus, attracting substantial external funding for its researchers. The university has also nurtured a thriving ecosystem of university spin-off companies and engineering firms.

University of Freiburg

With 180 undergraduate, graduate, and professional degree programs spread across 11 faculties, the University of Freiburg strongly emphasizes interdisciplinary and innovative studies. Students can enrich their bachelor's degree with a multidisciplinary year, fostering a well-rounded and forward-thinking educational experience.

Entry Requirements

Germany offers a limited selection of undergraduate courses solely taught in English. However, some programs provide instruction in German and English, offering an excellent opportunity for Bachelor's students to improve their German language skills while pursuing their studies. On the other hand, graduate students will find a growing array of English-taught degree options in Germany.

For admission to German universities, two main German language tests are universally accepted: the DSH (German language exam for university entrance), which is available only in Germany, and the TestDaF, which can be taken in 90 countries worldwide.

If you plan to enroll in a course partly taught in English, you must submit an English language certificate. The most popular English language proficiency tests accepted by German universities include PTE Academic, IELTS Academic, TOEFL iBT, and Duolingo.

Picking the Right Program

Discovering the right subject for your university program requires thoughtful consideration. Start by reflecting on your interests and passions. Identify the subjects that excited you the most during your high school years, as they can offer valuable insights into potential areas of study. Additionally, evaluate the field's worth in terms of the time and resources you'll invest, considering its relevance to your long-term goals and aspirations. Research the job prospects after completing the course to ensure they align with your career objectives.

Once you have narrowed down a subject, delve into the course content to ensure it covers topics that genuinely engage you and suit your learning style. If you're uncertain about a specific course, don't hesitate to contact the university for a copy of the syllabus or seek further information.

Beyond selecting a subject, you'll also need to determine the type of degree you want to pursue in higher education. Universities and colleges offer three main types of degrees: undergraduate (Bachelor's), graduate (Master's), and doctoral (PhD). Bachelor's degrees generally take three or four years, while master's degrees require one or two years of study. Doctoral programs can take up to five years, and they are ideal for those interested in research-oriented careers. Shorter courses like certificates and diplomas lasting less than a year are also available for specialized skill development. Choose the degree that best aligns with your career objectives and academic ambitions.

Scholarships

Friedrich Ebert Stiftung Scholarship:

The Friedrich Ebert Stiftung is a non-profit political foundation in Berlin, Germany, focusing on promoting social democracy both within the country and globally. The scholarship financially supports students who value social democracy and are pursuing undergraduate programs, graduate studies, or PhDs. It includes a monthly stipend of €774, study fee coverage of €300, health insurance contribution, and other benefits.

Heinrich Boll Scholarships for International Students:

The Heinrich Boll Foundation, an independent political foundation established in 1997, is committed to promoting political education in Germany and internationally. Their scholarship supports graduate students and PhD candidates with monthly stipends of €850 and €1200, respectively, enabling them to pursue their studies.

Konrad-Adenauer-Stiftung Scholarship:

The Konrad-Adenauer-Stiftung is a political foundation that fosters democracy, dialogue, and cooperation between Germany and other countries. The scholarship program supports students worldwide pursuing master's and doctoral degrees in Germany. It provides financial assistance, including monthly stipends of €861 for master's students and €1,200 for Ph.D. students, along with healthcare insurance, family allowance, and children's allowance.

Erasmus Scholarship Programs in Germany:

The Erasmus scholarship program offers full tuition and travel coverage to international postgraduate students pursuing master's degrees in Germany. This opportunity allows students to benefit from an international education experience.

Bayer Foundation Scholarship:

The Bayer Foundation offers scholarships to both domestic and international students pursuing master's and doctoral degrees in Germany. The scholarship, which can provide funding of up to $10,000, supports research in various critical areas of study.

Marie Curie International Incoming Fellowships (IIF) For Developing Countries:

This scholarship is open to international students pursuing a PhD in their respective fields. It offers funding of up to $15,000 per year to support students' research and education.

Mawista Scholarship:

Unlike traditional scholarships, the Mawista Scholarship focuses on supporting students who often receive less attention. It provides a one-time payment of $3,000 to students pursuing bachelor's, master's, and doctoral degrees.

Rosa Luxemburg Stiftung Scholarships for International Students:

The Rosa-Luxemburg-Stiftung Scholarship Department awards scholarships at all levels of education, including bachelor's, master's, and PhD's. Recipients are chosen based on their exceptional academic achievements, making it a prestigious opportunity for highly qualified students.

Deutschlandstipendium Program (DAAD Scholarship):

Funded by the federal government and private sponsors, the Deutschlandstipendium Program, or DAAD Scholarship, provides financial support to undergraduate and graduate students pursuing their studies in Germany. It includes a monthly allowance of €300.

DAAD Helmut-Schmidt Masters Scholarships for Public Policy and Good Governance:

The DAAD Helmut Schmidt Masters Scholarships for Public Policy and Good Governance Program is a government-funded scholarship opportunity for international students pursuing master's degrees in Germany. It offers full tuition fee coverage, a monthly allowance of 931 €, and additional benefits such as health insurance and travel fees.

Required Documents

Each university sets its admission criteria, but generally, most of the following will be included:

- Certified copy of a high-school diploma or a previously completed degree
- Translation of the course modules and grades
- Passport photo(s)
- Copy of your passport
- Proof of language proficiency – German and/or English

- Motivation letter
- Application fee

Citizenship / PR

Gaining German citizenship is not universally possible; it is contingent upon meeting specific conditions under three general instances. These occurrences are naturalization, right of blood (Jus Sanguinis), and right of soil (Jus Soli).

Citizenship by naturalization is attainable when an individual fulfills specific requirements set by the German government, making them eligible to apply for German citizenship. On the other hand, citizenship by right of blood or Jus Sanguinis applies to individuals who are direct descendants of German citizens, limited to their parents and excluding other relatives. Citizenship by right of soil or Jus Soli is acquired when an individual is born within the borders of Germany, on German soil.

For all individuals, except for EU, EEA, or Swiss nationals, fulfilling the prescribed requirements and fitting into one of these categories is essential to obtaining German citizenship. While these instances may seem straightforward, each has its distinct rules and regulations that must be carefully followed. It is important to note that gathering the necessary documentation and fulfilling all requirements within the designated timeframe can present significant challenges.

Job Opportunities

Germany boasts one of the most international economies globally, ranking alongside the USA, China, and Japan. As the top trading nation in the European Union, it is renowned for embracing innovation and facilitating international exports within its borders. The country's robust economy, exceptional infrastructure, and high-income levels make it a sought-after destination for foreigners, including international students.

Germany's allure also extends to expats, as many companies offer attractive employee benefits and perks that surpass those found in many other European nations. The country's job market provides excellent employment opportunities for individuals from all over the world.

Among the highest-paying professions in Germany are those in the medical, engineering, and financial sectors. Research indicates that the average annual salary for Germany's highest-paying jobs is at least €55,475.

As of 2023, here are the top 12 highest-paying jobs in Germany:

- Doctor
- Pilot
- Sales Manager
- Lawyer
- Portfolio Manager
- College Professor
- Engineering
- Software Developer
- Project Manager
- Risk Manager
- Judge
- Tax Advisor

These professions offer lucrative career paths for individuals seeking financial success and professional fulfillment in Germany's thriving job market.

Chapter 17:
Study Abroad Checklist for Italy

Italy's rich cultural heritage, encompassing art, architecture, cuisine, romanticism, and music, has profoundly influenced the global culture. The experience offers a unique opportunity to develop a broader world perspective and a deeper appreciation for different cultures, immersing oneself in an Italian study abroad,.

Italian culture embraces the tradition of "*riposo*," an afternoon break during the hottest part of the day when locals take a quick nap after lunch. This practice allows participants to understand and integrate into the local lifestyle.

Also, study abroad programs in Italy are highly sought-after due to the country's captivating food, scenic landscapes, historical sites, and world-renowned museums. Students can explore areas such as fashion, creative writing, visual art, and more with an extensive range of programs. The best study abroad programs cater to specific majors like communications, design, languages, medicine, and architecture.

For instance, a Florence study abroad program might offer humanities and social sciences courses, while a Rome study abroad program could provide enriching experiences in film and media studies.

Italy boasts a high-quality education system, hosting the prestigious University of Bologna, the oldest university globally, which has been a center of excellence for art, science, and higher education for centuries. The University of Padova is renowned for its science and engineering programs.

Additionally, even for non-language majors, learning another language, such as Italian, offers immense benefits. It enhances communication while traveling abroad and provides a competitive advantage in various fields, including foreign relations, tourism, and marketing.

Top Ten Universities

University of Bologna (Università di Bologna)

The University of Bologna, founded in 1088, is one of the world's oldest and most prestigious universities. It offers a wide range of programs and strongly emphasizes research and innovation. With its historic campus and esteemed faculty, the university attracts students from all over the globe.

University of Milan (Università degli Studi di Milano)

The University of Milan is renowned for its excellence in research and teaching across various disciplines. It was founded in 1924 and has since grown into one of Italy's leading universities, fostering a vibrant academic community and providing a diverse and challenging learning environment.

Sapienza University of Rome (Sapienza Università di Roma)

Sapienza is the largest university in Europe and one of the oldest in the world, dating back to 1303. Located in the heart of Rome, it boasts a rich academic tradition and offers a vast array of programs, attracting students from different cultural backgrounds.

Politecnico di Milano

Politecnico di Milano is a prominent technical university focusing on engineering, architecture, and design. It excels in research and industry collaborations, providing students with cutting-edge facilities and opportunities for practical experience.

University of Padua (Università degli Studi di Padova)

The University of Padua, founded in 1222, is another of Europe's oldest universities. It is known for its comprehensive research programs and outstanding contributions to various fields of study, including medicine, law, and the sciences.

University of Florence (Università degli Studi di Firenze)

The University of Florence is a leading institution in Italy, offering a wide range of arts, humanities, social sciences, and natural sciences programs. Its historic campus and vibrant cultural scene attract students seeking a dynamic learning experience.

University of Pisa (Università di Pisa)

The University of Pisa is renowned for its contributions to science and technology. It was founded in 1343 and has a strong reputation for research excellence in physics, engineering, and mathematics.

University of Turin (Università degli Studi di Torino)

The University of Turin is one of the oldest universities in Italy, dating back to 1404. It offers a wide array of programs and is notably recognized for its law, economics, and humanities research.

University of Naples Federico II (Università degli Studi di Napoli Federico II)

As one of the oldest public universities in the world (founded in 1224), the University of Naples Federico II boasts a rich history and a diverse range of academic programs, attracting students from various cultural backgrounds.

University of Trento (Università degli Studi di Trento)

The University of Trento is known for its high-quality teaching and research, especially in economics, social sciences, and information technology. It offers a welcoming and modern learning environment for students from Italy and abroad.

Entry Requirements

The entry requirements for Italian universities can vary depending on the level of study (undergraduate, postgraduate, or doctoral), the specific university and program, and whether the applicant is an EU/EEA/Swiss citizen or an international student. Below are the general entry requirements for each level of study:

Undergraduate (Bachelor's) Programs:

Academic Qualifications: Students must have completed their secondary education (high school or equivalent) and obtained a valid diploma that allows access to higher education in their home country.

Language Proficiency: For programs taught in Italian, students must demonstrate proficiency in the Italian language by providing an internationally recognized language certificate (e.g., CILS, CELI) or by passing a language test organized by the university. Some universities may offer undergraduate programs in English, and in such cases, students may need to provide proof of English proficiency (e.g., IELTS, TOEFL).

University Admission Test (if applicable): Some degree programs may require students to take an entrance exam or an assessment test to evaluate their aptitude and suitability for the course.

Postgraduate (Master's) Programs:

Academic Qualifications: Students must hold a relevant bachelor's degree or an equivalent qualification from a recognized institution. The degree should be related to the field of study they intend to pursue at the master's level.

Language Proficiency: Similar to undergraduate programs, language proficiency in Italian or English (depending on the language of instruction) is required.

Letters of Recommendation and Statement of Purpose: Many postgraduate programs require students to submit letters of recommendation from professors or employers and a statement of purpose explaining their academic and career goals.

Entrance Exam or Interview (if applicable): Some master's programs may have additional entry requirements, such as an entrance exam or an interview, to assess the candidate's knowledge and skills.

Finding the Right Program

Start by identifying your interests, strengths, and career aspirations. Consider what subjects you enjoy studying and what career path you envision for yourself. Understanding your passions and long-term goals will guide your program selection.

You can research the rankings and reputation of Italian universities and their specific programs. Look for universities known for excellence in your chosen field of study. Consider factors like faculty expertise, research opportunities, and industry partnerships.

It will help if you determine whether you are comfortable studying Italian or prefer an English-centric program. Many universities offer courses in English, especially at the postgraduate level, to cater to international students.

Review the curriculum of the programs you are interested in. Check if the courses offered align with your academic interests and if any specializations or concentrations match your career goals.

You have to ensure that the university and your chosen program are accredited and recognized nationally and internationally. Accredited programs generally meet specific quality standards.

Consider the location of the university and its proximity to amenities, cultural attractions, and potential job opportunities. Additionally, examine the available campus facilities, libraries, laboratories, and extracurricular activities.

Top Ten Scholarships

Italian Government Scholarships for Foreign Students

The Italian Ministry of Foreign Affairs offers scholarships to international students from various countries. These scholarships cover different academic levels, including undergraduate, postgraduate, and doctoral programs. They aim to promote cultural exchange and collaboration between Italy and other countries.

EDISU Piemonte Scholarships

EDISU Piemonte provides scholarships to domestic and international students studying at public universities in the Piedmont region of Italy. Scholarships are awarded based on financial need, academic merit, and other specific criteria.

Politecnico di Milano Scholarships

Politecnico di Milano, one of Italy's top technical universities, offers scholarships to international students pursuing undergraduate, master's, and doctoral programs. These scholarships may cover tuition fees, living expenses, or both.

Bocconi University Scholarships for International Students

Bocconi University in Milan offers various scholarships to outstanding international students applying to undergraduate, master's, and doctoral programs. These scholarships recognize academic excellence and may provide full or partial tuition waivers.

Università Cattolica del Sacro Cuore Scholarships

Università Cattolica del Sacro Cuore provides scholarships for international students who wish to study at the university's campuses in Milan, Piacenza, Cremona, and Rome. The scholarships are available for bachelor's and master's degree programs.

Scuola Normale Superiore PhD Scholarships

Scuola Normale Superiore (SNS) is a prestigious institution offering fully-funded PhD scholarships in various disciplines. These scholarships cover tuition fees, accommodation, and a stipend for living expenses.

University of Bologna Study Grants for International Students

The University of Bologna offers study grants and tuition fee waivers to deserving international students enrolled in bachelor's or master's programs.

Padua International Excellence Scholarship Program

The University of Padua offers scholarships to highly talented international students applying for degree programs. These scholarships support outstanding academic achievements and research potential.

NABA Scholarships for International Students

NABA (Nuova Accademia di Belle Arti) in Milan provides scholarships and financial aid to international students enrolling in design, fashion, and arts programs. These scholarships are merit-based.

Istituto Europeo di Design (IED) Scholarships

IED offers scholarships to international students pursuing various design courses at their campuses across Italy. Scholarships are awarded based on academic excellence and creative potential.

Required Documents

Application Form: Complete and submit the university's official application form for the desired program of study.

Academic Transcripts: You must provide official transcripts or academic records from your previous educational institutions, including high school for undergraduate applicants and bachelor's degree for postgraduate applicants.

Diploma or Degree Certificate: A copy of your high school diploma or bachelor's degree certificate, depending on the level of study you are applying for.

Language Proficiency Test Results: Proof of language proficiency in either Italian or English, depending on the language of instruction of your chosen program. This may include language test scores such as TOEFL or IELTS for English and CILS or CELI for Italian.

Passport or Identity Document: You must submit a copy of a valid passport or identification document to verify your identity and nationality.

Passport-sized Photographs: Provide recent passport-sized photographs per the university's specifications.

Specific requirements may vary from one university to another or even between different programs within the same university.

Citizenship / PR

The process for obtaining Italian citizenship can be complex and may vary based on your circumstances. There are different ways to acquire Italian citizenship, including by descent (jure sanguinis), marriage to an Italian citizen, naturalization, or through special provisions for certain groups (e.g., stateless individuals or refugees). There are different ways to obtain citizenship in Italy:

Citizenship by Descent (Jure Sanguinis):

If you have Italian ancestors, you may be eligible for citizenship by descent. The process involves proving your lineage through birth certificates, marriage certificates, and other relevant documents, usually dating back to the Italian ancestor. Requirements and eligibility criteria may differ depending on the generation and the date of emigration of your Italian ancestor.

Citizenship by Marriage:

If you are married to an Italian citizen, you may be eligible for citizenship after a certain period of marriage, usually two years if you reside in Italy or three years if you live abroad. You must meet specific requirements and demonstrate sufficient knowledge of the Italian language.

Citizenship by Naturalization:

Foreign nationals legally residing in Italy for a certain period (usually ten years, but it may vary based on circumstances) may be eligible for citizenship by naturalization. During this period, you must have a valid residence permit and demonstrate integration into Italian society, knowledge of the Italian language, and sufficient financial stability.

It's important to note that Italian citizenship laws are subject to change, and the requirements can be complex, depending on your situation. Therefore, it is highly recommended to seek professional advice from an immigration lawyer or consult the official website of the Italian Ministry of Foreign Affairs for the most up-to-date and accurate information regarding the citizenship process.

Job Opportunities

Italy offers a diverse range of job opportunities across various industries. Some of the key sectors with employment opportunities in Italy include:

Tourism and Hospitality

Italy is a top tourist destination with a rich cultural heritage and picturesque landscapes. Job opportunities are available in hotels, restaurants, tour agencies, and other tourism-related businesses.

Manufacturing

Italy has a strong manufacturing industry known for luxury fashion, automotive, machinery, and design. Jobs are available in production, engineering, design, and management roles.

Finance and Banking

As a major financial hub, Milan offers job opportunities in the banking, finance, investment, and insurance sectors.

Information Technology (IT) and Software Development

With a growing tech sector, cities like Milan and Turin have job openings in IT, software development, data analytics, and cybersecurity.

Healthcare and Life Sciences

There is a demand for healthcare professionals in hospitals, clinics, research institutions, and pharmaceutical companies.

Education and Language Teaching

English teaching jobs are available in language schools and universities, and there is also demand for teachers in other subjects.

Art and Design

Italy's rich artistic and design heritage creates opportunities in the art, fashion, and interior design industries.

Green Energy and Sustainability

As the country focuses on renewable energy and sustainability, there are opportunities in environmental engineering and green technology sectors.

Chapter 18:

Study Abroad Checklist for Spain

Every year, thousands of students from across the world go to Spain to attend one of the 76 universities in the country. They come to Spain for numerous reasons, with the knowledge that studying here is a truly enlightening experience. Spain allows its international students to create new attitudes and concepts about life. It gives students a fresh perspective on the world around them.

Spain has a rich, diverse culture with a long history, vibrant traditions, and a lively arts scene. Studying there allows you to immerse yourself in this culture, learn the language, and gain a deeper understanding of Spanish history and way of life.

Spanish is one of the world's most widely spoken languages. Studying in Spain provides an immersive environment to improve your language skills, which can be incredibly valuable personally and professionally. Spain is home to several renowned universities and educational institutions. You can access high-quality academic programs and courses, often with a unique European perspective.

Spain also offers diverse study programs across various disciplines, including art, history, science, engineering, business, and more. This diversity allows you to find a program that aligns with your academic and career goals.

Studying abroad exposes you to a global network of students and professionals. Building these international connections can be advantageous for future career opportunities and collaborations.

Top Ten Universities

University of Barcelona (Universitat de Barcelona)

One of Spain's oldest universities, the University of Barcelona is known for its extensive research initiatives and diverse academic programs. It's located in the vibrant city of Barcelona and offers a wide range of disciplines for local and international students.

Complutense University of Madrid (Universidad Complutense de Madrid)

Located in the heart of Madrid, this university is one of Spain's largest and most prestigious. It offers a wide array of programs and strongly emphasizes research, making it a hub for academic innovation.

Autonomous University of Barcelona (Universitat Autònoma de Barcelona)

Known for its beautiful campus and strong research focus, this university offers diverse academic programs. It's located near Barcelona and is well-regarded for contributing to various fields.

Pompeu Fabra University (Universitat Pompeu Fabra)

This relatively young university has quickly gained recognition for its high-quality teaching and research. It's known for its strong emphasis on social sciences, humanities, and communication studies.

University of Navarra (Universidad de Navarra)

Situated in Pamplona, this private university is recognized for its rigorous academic programs and commitment to research. It's particularly renowned for its business, law, and communication faculties.

University of Granada (Universidad de Granada)

With a rich history dating back to the Renaissance, this university is known for its academic excellence and cultural significance. It's situated in Granada and offers a wide range of disciplines.

Carlos III University of Madrid (Universidad Carlos III de Madrid)

This modern university strongly emphasizes social sciences and humanities, offering innovative programs in law, economics, and political science. It's known for its dynamic and international student body.

University of Valencia (Universitat de València)

Established in the early 16th century, this university is one of the oldest in Spain. It's recognized for its contributions to science, arts, and humanities, and its campus offers a blend of historical and modern architecture.

IE University

A private institution with campuses in Madrid and Segovia, IE University is known for its business, law, and social sciences programs. It focuses on providing a dynamic and international learning environment.

Polytechnic University of Catalonia (Universitat Politècnica de Catalunya)

Specializing in engineering, architecture, and technology, this university is a technical education and research leader. It has multiple campuses and contributes significantly to advancements in these fields.

Entry Requirements

Entry requirements for Spanish universities can vary depending on the level of study (undergraduate or postgraduate) and the specific university or program you're applying to. But here are the general entry requirements you can expect:

Undergraduate Programs

You'll typically need a high school diploma or an equivalent qualification from your country. This is the basic educational requirement for admission.

If the program is taught in Spanish, you might need to demonstrate your proficiency in the language. This is usually done through standardized tests like the DELE (Diploma of Spanish as a Foreign Language) or the Test of Spanish as a Foreign Language (Prueba de Acceso a la Universidad, or PAU).

Some programs or universities might require you to take entrance exams, especially for competitive programs like medicine or engineering. You must apply through the university's admissions portal, providing your educational history, personal statement, and any other required documents.

Postgraduate Programs (Master's and PhD)

You'll need a recognized bachelor's degree or an equivalent qualification from an accredited institution. Like undergraduate programs, if your chosen program is taught in Spanish, you might need to prove your language proficiency through tests like DELE or PAU.

You'll likely need to provide official transcripts from your previous education and letters of recommendation. Many postgraduate programs require a statement of purpose outlining your academic and professional goals and how the program aligns with them.

Depending on the program, you might need to take specific entrance exams or attend interviews as part of the selection process. If applying for a PhD, you might need to submit a research proposal outlining your intended research topic and approach. Apply through the university's admissions portal, providing all required documents and information.

Finding the Right Program

When embarking on the journey of finding the perfect study program in Spanish universities, a systematic approach ensures you make an informed decision tailored to your ambitions and aspirations.

Begin with a thorough self-assessment, delving into your interests and career goals. Reflect upon subjects that genuinely captivate and align with your envisioned career path. Simultaneously, take stock of your academic strengths and areas where you aspire to further develop your skills. This introspective phase forms the foundation of your exploration.

Moving into the research phase, immerse yourself in the websites of Spanish universities. Navigate through the virtual corridors of their offerings, faculty profiles, and facilities. As you scout for programs, align them with your interests and academic objectives. Embrace the diversity of options, exploring both specialized courses and those that foster interdisciplinary learning. While exploring, prioritize accredited institutions with a strong reputation in your chosen field. While not definitive, university rankings can offer insights into overall institutional recognition.

Language of instruction plays a pivotal role. Ascertain whether your preferred program is delivered in English or Spanish. In the latter case, evaluate your current language proficiency and willingness to enhance it for successful integration.

Delve into admission requirements. Each program may stipulate distinct prerequisites encompassing academic qualifications, entrance exams, recommendation letters, and supplementary documents. Adhering to these requirements is vital for a seamless application process.

The geographical context of the university is also significant. Reflect on the city and region that will shape your academic journey. Consider aspects such as the climate, cost of living, cultural offerings, and potential career prospects. Financial considerations go hand in hand. Estimate tuition costs, living expenses, and additional fees. Simultaneously, research scholarships, grants, and financial aid options that cater to international students.

Engage with advisors for informed decisions. Seek counsel from school counselors, educators, or education consultants. Their expertise aligns your academic background and goals with program choices.

Scholarships

Erasmus+ Scholarship

The Erasmus+ program offers scholarships for students to study abroad in European countries, including Spain. It aims to promote international mobility and collaboration among European universities.

La Caixa Foundation Scholarship

The La Caixa Foundation provides scholarships for postgraduate studies, including master's and doctoral programs, in Spain. These scholarships are highly competitive and support academic excellence.

Spanish Government Scholarships (Becas MAEC-AECID)

Offered by the Spanish Ministry of Foreign Affairs, European Union, and Cooperation, these scholarships are designed for international students pursuing postgraduate studies, research, and cultural exchanges in Spain.

ICETEX Scholarship for Colombian Students

This scholarship is specifically for Colombian students who wish to study in Spain. It is funded by the Colombian Institute of Educational Credit and Technical Studies Abroad (ICETEX).

DAAD Scholarship for Spanish Universities

The German Academic Exchange Service (DAAD) provides scholarships for German students to study in Spain. These scholarships cover various fields and academic levels.

Agencia Española de Cooperación Internacional (AECID) Scholarships

AECID offers a range of scholarships for students from developing countries to pursue higher education and research in Spain. These scholarships focus on development-related disciplines.

University-Specific Scholarships

Many Spanish universities offer their own scholarships for international students. These scholarships could cover tuition fees, living expenses, or a combination of both. Check the websites of your chosen universities for details.

Santander Scholarships

Santander Bank collaborates with various universities to offer scholarships to international students studying in Spain. These scholarships often aim to support mobility, research, or academic excellence.

Fulbright Program in Spain

The Fulbright Program offers scholarships for U.S. citizens to study, teach, or research in Spain. It fosters cultural exchange and academic collaboration between the U.S. and Spain.

European Union Scholarships for Developing Countries

The European Union offers scholarships for students from developing countries through various programs like Erasmus Mundus. These scholarships support academic mobility and capacity building.

Required Documents

- Application Form
- Educational Documents:
- High School Diploma or Equivalent
- Bachelor's Degree Certificate
- Transcripts
- Language Proficiency
- Curriculum Vitae (CV) or Resume
- Statement of Purpose (SOP) or Personal Statement
- Letters of Recommendation
- Passport Copy
- Passport-Sized Photographs

- Application Fee
- Entrance Exam Scores
- Portfolio (if applicable)
- Proof of Financial Support
- Health Insurance

Citizenship / PR

The citizenship process in Spain involves several steps and requirements for individuals who wish to become Spanish citizens. It's important to note that the process can be complex and may change over time, so it's advisable to consult official government sources or legal professionals for the most up-to-date information.

Residency Requirements:

To apply for Spanish citizenship, you typically must have legally resided in Spain for a certain period. The residency requirement may vary depending on your circumstances, such as whether you are from a Spanish-speaking country or if you are a refugee.

Legal Residency Status:

You need to have legal residency status in Spain. This usually means having a valid residence permit or similar authorization to live in Spain.

Language Proficiency:

Depending on your circumstances, you may need to demonstrate a certain level of proficiency in Spanish. This requirement can be waived for citizens of Spanish-speaking countries.

Integration and Cultural Knowledge:

Applicants may need to demonstrate their integration into Spanish society and show an understanding of Spanish culture, history, and social values.

Renunciation of Previous Citizenship:

Spain generally requires applicants to renounce their previous citizenship(s) as part of the process. However, some countries allow dual citizenship, so it's important to understand the rules in your home country.

Background Checks and Character Requirements:

Spanish authorities conduct background checks and assess the applicant's character, criminal history, and overall behavior.

Documentation:

You will need to provide various documents, such as birth certificates, marriage certificates (if applicable), proof of residence, language proficiency certificates, and other relevant paperwork.

Application Submission:

Once you have met the requirements, you can submit your citizenship application to the relevant authorities. The application process includes filling out forms and providing the required documentation.

Processing and Approval:

After submitting your application, it will be reviewed by the appropriate authorities. The processing time can vary, and you may be required to attend interviews or provide additional information.

Oath of Allegiance:

If your application is approved, you must take an oath of allegiance to Spain.

Citizenship Grant and Documentation:

Upon completing the process successfully, you will be granted Spanish citizenship. You will receive a naturalization certificate and can apply for a Spanish passport.

Job Opportunities

Spain offers a variety of job opportunities across different industries, but the specific job market can fluctuate based on economic conditions and other factors.

Tourism and Hospitality

Spain is a popular tourist destination, leading to hotels, restaurants, travel agencies, and related service opportunities.

Technology and IT

Spain has a growing tech sector, particularly in cities like Barcelona and Madrid, offering software development, data analysis, and IT services positions.

Engineering and Construction

With ongoing infrastructure projects and urban development, there's a demand for civil engineers, architects, and construction professionals.

Healthcare

There is a need for healthcare professionals, including doctors, nurses, and medical staff, in both the public and private sectors.

Finance and Banking

Metropolitan cities like Madrid have a strong financial sector, providing opportunities in banking, finance, and related services.

Manufacturing and Automotive

Spain is known for its automotive industry, with companies like Seat, and also has a presence in manufacturing, offering roles in engineering, production, and logistics.

Agribusiness

The agriculture sector offers farming, food production, and related industries opportunities.

Language Services

English language proficiency is valuable in roles related to translation, interpretation, content creation, and language training.

Creative Industries

Spain has a rich cultural scene, including design, fashion, media, and arts, providing opportunities for creative professionals.

Consulting and Business Services

Management consulting, business analysis, and professional services sectors also offer employment options.

It's important to note that job availability can vary by region. Larger cities like Madrid, Barcelona, Valencia, and Bilbao tend to offer more job opportunities due to their economic and cultural significance. Fluency in Spanish is often an advantage, especially for roles involving communication with local clients and colleagues.

Chapter 19:
Study Abroad Checklist for France

Studying abroad in France offers a captivating array of benefits that extend far beyond the classroom, making it an enriching and transformative experience. Immerse yourself in a culture renowned for its rich history, art, and cuisine, gaining a profound understanding of global perspectives. Engaging with the vibrant local communities and mastering the French language enhances your communication skills and fosters a sense of adaptability and cross-cultural competence, invaluable traits in today's interconnected world.

The country's esteemed educational institutions provide top-notch academic opportunities, nurturing intellectual growth and offering diverse courses that span disciplines. Moreover, the strategic location within Europe makes exploring neighboring countries convenient, opening doors to a continent steeped in diverse traditions and landscapes. As you navigate daily life amidst architectural marvels and picturesque landscapes, you'll develop independence and resilience, honing personal and academic skills that will undoubtedly set you apart in your future endeavors.

Embarking on this journey, you'll broaden your horizons and carry the essence of France's charm with you, fostering a global perspective that extends far beyond your time abroad.

Top 10 Universities

Sorbonne University

With a history of over 750 years, Sorbonne University is a prestigious institution known for its strong emphasis on humanities, social sciences, and natural sciences. It offers a wide range of programs and boasts a rich academic tradition.

École Normale (ENS Paris)

ENS Paris is renowned for its rigorous academic environment and selectivity. It is mainly known for producing eminent scholars and researchers across various fields, including science, humanities, and social sciences.

École Polytechnique

Often referred to as "X," École Polytechnique is a prestigious engineering school known for its rigorous education and strong focus on mathematics and sciences. It has a reputation for producing top-notch engineers and scientists.

Pierre and Marie Curie University (UPMC)

A leading institution in science and medicine, UPMC is named after the famous physicists Pierre and Marie Curie. It offers a wide range of programs in various scientific disciplines.

Paris Sciences et Lettres (PSL) University

PSL is a collective of renowned institutions, including École Normale Supérieure Collège de France. It offers interdisciplinary programs and is known for fostering innovation and creativity.

HEC Paris

HEC Paris is a prestigious business school recognized for its MBA and executive education programs. It has a strong international reputation is known for producing successful business leaders.

University of Paris-Sud (Paris 11)

Paris-Sud is a leading research-oriented institution known for its excellence in science and technology. It has a strong focus on physics, chemistry, and engineering disciplines.

Sciences Po Paris

Specialized in social sciences and political studies, Sciences Po is renowned for emphasizing critical thinking and international relations. It prepares students for careers in politics, diplomacy, and academia.

University of Strasbourg

As one of the oldest universities in the world, the University of Strasbourg has a rich history. It offers a diverse range of programs and is known for its strong focus on research and innovation.

L'Université Grenoble Alpes

This university is recognized for its science, engineering, and technology strengths. It is situated in the heart of the French Alps, providing a unique environment for academic and outdoor pursuits.

Entry Requirements

University entry requirements in France can vary depending on the level of study (undergraduate or postgraduate), the specific program you're applying to, and the university itself. Here is a general overview of the typical entry requirements for both undergraduate and postgraduate programs in France:

Undergraduate Programs:

High School Diploma or Equivalent: To be eligible for undergraduate programs, you need to have completed a high school diploma or an equivalent qualification in your home country.

Language Proficiency: Many programs in France are taught in French. If your chosen program is in French, you'll likely need to demonstrate proficiency by submitting a standardized language test score like the DELF/DALF or TCF.

Application through Parcoursup: You'll need to apply through the Parcoursup platform for most undergraduate programs, including public universities. This centralized application system allows you to apply to multiple universities and programs.

Postgraduate Programs:

Bachelor's Degree or Equivalent: To be eligible for a master's program in France, you'll generally need a bachelor's degree or equivalent from a recognized institution.

Language Proficiency: Similar to undergraduate programs, language proficiency is vital if your chosen program is taught in French. Alternatively, if your program is in English, you might need to provide proof of English language proficiency through tests like TOEFL or IELTS.

Academic Transcripts and References: You'll typically need to provide academic transcripts and possibly letters of recommendation to support your application.

Application through Various Platforms: Postgraduate applications might be submitted through different platforms, depending on the university and program. Some common platforms include the university's application portal or platforms like Campus France.

It's important to note that entry requirements vary widely between universities and programs. The competitive nature of certain programs might mean that meeting the minimum requirements does not guarantee admission. It is crucial to research the specific program and university you're interested in and check their official websites for detailed admission criteria.

Finding the Right Program

Finding the perfect study program in France is all about careful research and thoughtful decision-making to ensure the program fits your educational and career dreams.

First, consider what you want to achieve academically and in your future job. Do you have a specific subject in mind? Are you aiming for a bachelor's, master's, or PhD? Pinpointing your goals will make your search more focused.

Next, look into French universities that offer programs related to your interests. It is a good idea to choose well-known academic institutions with strong academic reputations in the chosen field.

Decide if you'd like to study in French or English. Many universities offer both language options, so you can pick the one that matches your language skills.

Use online resources like Campus France to learn about studying in France. Also, visit university websites to get details about their programs.

Search engines designed to find programs (like Campus France, Eduniversal, and MastersPortal) are helpful. They let you filter and compare programs based on your preferences.

While rankings aren't the only thing to consider, they can give you an idea of program quality. Check out respected ranking lists like QS World University Rankings or Times Higher Education.

Read the program descriptions carefully to understand what each course covers. Make sure it lines up with your interests.

Look into the requirements for admission. Make sure you have the proper academic background and language skills. Some programs might need extra materials, like a statement about your goals or examples of your work.

You can also contact advisors at universities or French consulates in your country. They can help you understand your options and guide you through the application process.

Based on your research, make a shortlist of programs that match your goals and preferences. When you're ready, start applying to the programs you like. Get all the necessary documents ready and meet the application deadlines.

Remember to stay open-minded. Sometimes, you'll find great opportunities in places you didn't initially consider.

Scholarships

Eiffel Excellence Scholarship Program

The Eiffel Excellence Scholarship Program is a competitive scholarship offered by the French Ministry for Europe and Foreign Affairs. It supports international students pursuing master's and doctoral degrees in various fields, including engineering, economics, and social sciences. The scholarship covers tuition fees, living expenses, and international travel.

French Government Scholarships (Eiffel Campus France Scholarships)

The French Government offers a range of scholarships through the Eiffel Campus France program to international students at the master's and PhD levels. These scholarships cover tuition fees, a monthly stipend, and other benefits. The program aims to attract high-achieving students to study in France.

Erasmus+ Scholarships

Erasmus+ is a European Union program that offers scholarships to students for international study and mobility. It provides funding for exchange programs, internships, and joint master's degrees across participating European universities, including those in France.

Charpak Scholarship

The Charpak Scholarship, offered by the Embassy of France in India, supports Indian students who wish to pursue higher education in France. The scholarship is available for master's and PhD programs and covers tuition fees, living expenses, and health insurance.

Ampère Excellence Scholarships

The ENS de Lyon awards the Ampère Excellence Scholarships to outstanding international students interested in pursuing master's or doctoral programs. The scholarship covers tuition fees and provides a monthly stipend.

A*Midex Scholarship

The A*Midex Scholarship is available to international students at Aix-Marseille University. It supports students pursuing master's or PhD degrees in areas related to the university's research themes. The scholarship covers tuition fees and provides a stipend.

INSEAD Scholarships

INSEAD, a renowned business school, offers various scholarships to support students in its MBA, EMBA, and other programs. Scholarships are awarded based on merit, diversity, and need. They cover tuition fees or living expenses.

Aga Khan Foundation Scholarship

The Aga Khan Foundation offers scholarships for postgraduate studies to outstanding students from developing countries, including those in France. The scholarship aims to support scholars who have exceptional academic records and demonstrate leadership potential.

Campus France Scholarships

Campus France provides information about a range of scholarships available to international students in France. These scholarships are offered by various organizations, including governments, universities, and private foundations, and cover various disciplines and degree levels.

Rhône-Alpes Scholarships

The Rhône-Alpes region in France offers scholarships to international students who wish to pursue higher education in the region. These scholarships are available at various universities and institutions in the area and are designed to support academic excellence.

Required Documents

Undergraduate Applications:

Application Form: Complete and submit the university's online application form.

High School Transcripts: Official transcripts of your secondary education (high school) showing your grades and courses.

High School Diploma: A copy of your high school diploma or leaving certificate.

Language Proficiency: Proof of language proficiency, usually in French (DELF/DALF) or English (TOEFL/IELTS) if your program is in that language.

Personal Statement: A statement of purpose outlining your academic interests, motivations, and why you want to study the chosen program.

Letters of Recommendation: One or more letters of recommendation from teachers or counselors who can speak to your academic abilities and character.

Passport Copy: A copy of your passport or identification document.

CV/Resume: A summary of your educational background, extracurricular activities, and relevant work experience.

Application Fee: Some universities may require an application fee.

Postgraduate Applications:

Application Form: Complete and submit the university's online application form.

Bachelor's Degree Transcripts: Official transcripts of your completed bachelor's degree, showing your grades and courses.

Bachelor's Degree Certificate: A copy of your bachelor's degree certificate.

Language Proficiency: Proof of language proficiency in the language of instruction (French or English).

Curriculum Vitae (CV): A detailed resume highlighting your academic achievements, work experience, and any research or publications.

Statement of Purpose: A statement outlining your academic and professional goals, why you're interested in the program, and how it aligns with your aspirations.

Letters of Recommendation: Typically, two or three letters of recommendation from professors or professionals who can vouch for your abilities.

Passport Copy: A copy of your passport or identification document.

GRE/GMAT Scores (if required): Some programs might require standardized test scores like GRE or GMAT.

France offers a variety of English-taught programs to help students improve their language proficiency. These programs are designed for individuals who want to study English or other subjects in English while immersing themselves in French culture. Here are some options:

University Programs: Many universities in France offer English-taught bachelor's, master's, and doctoral programs in a wide range of fields, including business, engineering, humanities, and social sciences. Examples include Sciences Po in Paris and INSEAD.

Language Schools: Language schools and institutes in France offer English language courses for international students. These programs are often intensive and can range from a few weeks to several months. Examples include Alliance Française and EF Education First.

Summer Language Programs: Several universities and language schools offer summer English language and culture programs. These programs are typically shorter in duration and may include cultural activities and excursions.

TEFL/TESOL Certification Programs: If you want to teach English as a foreign language, you can enroll in a TEFL (Teaching

English as a Foreign Language) or TESOL (Teaching English to Speakers of Other Languages) certification program in France.

Exchange Programs: Some universities in France have exchange agreements with institutions in English-speaking countries. These programs allow students to spend a semester or academic year studying in an English-speaking environment while earning credit toward their degree.

Language Immersion Programs: Some language schools and organizations offer language immersion programs where you live with a host family and attend language classes. This provides a complete immersion experience in English.

PR / Citizenship

Acquiring citizenship in France, also known as French nationality, involves a legal process and specific eligibility criteria. Citizenship can be obtained through various means, including birth, marriage, naturalization, and more.

Birth in France:

If you are born in France to at least one parent who is a French citizen, you automatically acquire French nationality.

Birth to French Parents Abroad:

You may be eligible for French citizenship if you are born abroad to French parents. The rules can be complex and depend on factors like the parents' nationality, the country of birth, and whether the French parent(s) were born in France or acquired citizenship.

Marriage to a French Citizen:

If you are married to a French citizen and have lived in France for a certain period, you may be eligible to apply for French citizenship. The duration of marriage and residence requirements can vary.

Naturalization:

Naturalization is the process of acquiring French citizenship through an application. The requirements for naturalization include:

Residence Requirement: You must have lived legally in France for a specific period, usually five years. For some instances, this requirement can be shorter, such as for refugees or spouses of French citizens.

Integration: You should demonstrate a commitment to integrating into French society, including language proficiency, knowledge of French culture, and respect for French values.

Stable Income: You should have a steady source of income to support yourself and any dependents.

No Criminal Record: You should have a clean criminal record.

Renunciation of Previous Citizenship: France generally requires that you renounce your previous citizenship(s) upon obtaining French citizenship. However, there are exceptions, such as cases where it's impossible to reject due to the laws of your home country.

Special Cases:

There are additional pathways to citizenship for certain individuals, including refugees, stateless persons, and individuals who have rendered exceptional services to France.

Job Opportunities

France offers a diverse range of job opportunities across various sectors and industries. As one of the world's largest economies, it has a robust job market that caters to different skill sets and career aspirations.

Information Technology (IT) and Tech Industries:

France has a growing tech sector, especially in cities like Paris and Lyon. Jobs in software development, cybersecurity, data analysis, artificial intelligence (AI), and tech startups are available.

Engineering and Manufacturing:

France has a strong manufacturing sector with companies producing automobiles, aerospace products, machinery, and more. Opportunities exist for engineers, technicians, and production specialists.

Healthcare and Life Sciences:

The healthcare and pharmaceutical industries offer job opportunities for doctors, nurses, researchers, pharmacists, and medical technology and biotechnology professionals.

Tourism and Hospitality:

France's tourism industry is renowned globally. Jobs in this sector include hospitality management, tourism promotion, hotel operations, and restaurant services.

Education and Research:

France has prestigious universities and research institutions that offer teaching and research positions. Opportunities exist for professors, researchers, and academic administrators.

Consulting and Professional Services:

Consulting firms provide services in management, strategy, and various business functions. Job roles include management consultants, business analysts, and financial advisors.

Fashion and Luxury Goods:

France is a fashion hub with renowned luxury brands. Job opportunities are available in design, marketing, retail, and production.

Media and Entertainment:

The media industry in France includes film, television, publishing, and advertising. Opportunities are available for journalists, editors, producers, and creative professionals.

Language Teaching:

As a non-French speaker, teaching your native language (such as English) is a potential job opportunity, especially in language schools and institutes.

Remember that the job market can be competitive, and language skills, especially French, are often crucial for many roles, especially those involving interactions with the local population. Networking, researching companies, and understanding the job requirements are vital to securing employment in France. Additionally, considering factors like cost of living, work permits, and visa regulations is essential if you are an expatriate seeking work in the country.

Chapter 20:

Study Abroad Checklist for Hungary

Hungary is known for its high-quality education system. The country has a long tradition of academic excellence and is home to several reputable universities. Many programs are taught in English, making it accessible to international students. Hungary offers relatively affordable tuition fees for EU and non-EU students compared to many Western European countries. This makes it an attractive destination for students looking for quality education at a reduced cost.

Hungarian universities offer various academic programs, including arts and humanities, sciences, engineering, medicine, business, and more. You can find programs at the undergraduate, master's, and doctoral levels. Also, its central location in Europe makes it a melting pot of cultures. Studying in Hungary allows you to interact with people from diverse backgrounds and gain a global perspective.

This country has a rich cultural heritage, includes historical landmarks, museums, and festivals. It's an excellent place to explore European history and culture while you study. While Hungarian is the official language, many Hungarians speak English and other languages, especially in urban areas. This can make daily life and communication accessible for international students.

Hungary is actively involved in international research collaborations, and its universities offer research opportunities for students interested in various fields.

Also, Hungary is a member of the European Union, making studying there easier for EU students. It also allows students to travel and explore other EU countries without additional visas.

While studying here offers many advantages, it's essential to research specific universities and programs to find the one that best aligns with your academic and personal goals.

Top Ten Universities

Eötvös Loránd University (ELTE)

ELTE is one of Hungary's oldest and most prestigious universities in Budapest. It offers a wide range of programs and is known for its strong academic traditions.

Central European University (CEU)

CEU is an international institution with campuses in Budapest and Vienna. It specializes in social sciences, humanities, and public policy and is known for its commitment to academic freedom and research.

University of Debrecen

The University of Debrecen, located in Debrecen, is one of the leading universities in Hungary. It offers diverse programs and is renowned for its medical and agricultural faculties.

Budapest University of Technology and Economics (BME)

BME is the oldest technical university in Hungary and offers engineering, technology, and natural sciences programs. It is located in Budapest and has a strong reputation in STEM fields.

University of Szeged

The University of Szeged, situated in Szeged, is known for its research excellence and offers various academic programs. It has a strong emphasis on international collaboration.

Semmelweis University

Located in Budapest, Semmelweis University is renowned for its medical and health sciences programs. It is one of the oldest medical schools in Europe and offers high-quality healthcare education.

Corvinus University of Budapest

Corvinus University is known for its economics, business, and social sciences programs. It is located in Budapest and has a strong focus on internationalization.

University of Pécs

The University of Pécs, located in Pécs, offers diverse programs and is known for its strong emphasis on research and internationalization.

University of Miskolc

The University of Miskolc is situated in Miskolc and specializes in engineering, technology, and natural sciences. It is known for its contributions to industrial and technical research.

Budapest Business School (BBS)

BBS is one of Hungary's leading institutions for business and economics education. It offers a range of business-related programs and is based in Budapest.

Entry Requirements

Entry requirements for Hungarian universities may vary depending on the level of study (bachelor's, master's, or doctoral), the specific university and program, and whether you are an EU or non-EU student.

For Undergraduate (Bachelor's) Programs:

- You will typically need to complete a secondary education program and possess a high school diploma or equivalent. The specific requirements may vary by program, so you must check with the university you're interested in.
- If your chosen program is taught in English, you may need to demonstrate proficiency in the English language through standardized tests such as IELTS or TOEFL. Some universities may also accept English proficiency certificates issued by the institution.
- In some cases, universities may require you to take an entrance examination or participate in an interview as part of the admission process, particularly for competitive programs like medicine or architecture.
- You must complete the university's application form and submit all required documents by the specified deadline. Application forms are usually available on the university's website.
- You must provide copies of your high school transcripts and certificates to demonstrate your academic qualifications.
- Non-EU students may need to demonstrate that they have sufficient financial resources to cover their living expenses while studying in Hungary.

For Postgraduate (Master's and Doctoral) Programs:

- You will typically need a relevant bachelor's degree or equivalent for admission to a master's program. For doctoral programs, you will usually need a master's degree or equivalent.
- If the program is taught in English, you may need to provide proof of English proficiency through tests like IELTS or TOEFL. Some universities may also offer language assessments as part of the admission process.

- Some programs, especially competitive ones, may require you to take entrance exams or participate in interviews to assess your suitability for the program.
- You will need to provide copies of your academic transcripts and certificates, including those from your bachelor's or master's programs.
- If you are applying for a doctoral program, you may need to submit a proposal outlining your intended research topic and methodology.
- Many postgraduate programs require a letter of recommendation from professors or professionals who can vouch for your academic or professional qualifications.
- Complete the university's application form and adhere to all submission deadlines.

Please note that entry requirements can vary significantly between universities and programs, so it's crucial to check the specific requirements for the program you are interested in on the university's official website or contact the university's admissions office for detailed and up-to-date information. Additionally, immigration and visa requirements may apply, especially for non-EU students, so it's essential to inquire about these.

Scholarships

Stipendium Hungaricum Scholarship:

The Stipendium Hungaricum Scholarship is a fully-funded scholarship program the Hungarian government offers to international students from various countries. It covers tuition fees, accommodation, and a monthly stipend for bachelor's, master's, and doctoral programs at Hungarian universities.

Central European University (CEU) Scholarships:

CEU offers various scholarships, including merit-based and need-based awards, to support international students pursuing master's and doctoral programs in social sciences, humanities, law, and public policy.

Erasmus+ Scholarships:

Erasmus+ is an EU-funded program that provides scholarships and grants for European and international students to study in Hungary and other European countries. It supports both short-term exchanges and full-degree programs.

Eötvös Loránd University (ELTE) Scholarships:

ELTE offers several scholarships and tuition fee waivers for talented international students, including the ELTE Excellence Scholarship and ELTE Science and Innovation Scholarship.

Hungarian Scholarship Board Scholarships:

The Hungarian Scholarship Board (MAB) offers scholarships to international students for bachelor's, master's, and doctoral studies in Hungary. These scholarships cover tuition fees and provide a stipend.

Visegrad Fund Scholarships:

The International Visegrad Fund provides scholarships for students from Visegrad Group countries (Czech Republic, Hungary, Poland, Slovakia) to study in any of these countries. It supports bachelor's, master's, and doctoral studies.

University-Specific Scholarships:

Many Hungarian universities offer scholarships and financial aid to international students. These scholarships may be based on academic excellence, specific programs, or diversity and may vary from one university to another.

DAAD Scholarships:

The German Academic Exchange Service (DAAD) offers scholarships for German students to study in Hungary and vice versa. These scholarships support various academic levels and fields of study.

Fulbright Scholarships:

The Fulbright Program offers scholarships for U.S. citizens to conduct research, teach, or pursue graduate studies in Hungary. It promotes academic and cultural exchange between the United States and Hungary.

Scholarship Programs from Home Countries:

Some governments and organizations from other countries offer scholarships for their citizens to study in Hungary. Examples include the Chinese Government Scholarship, Turkish Scholarships, and more.

Required Documents

- Ensure your passport is valid for the entire duration of your intended stay in Hungary and has at least one blank page for visa stamps.
- You may need a student visa to enter Hungary, depending on your nationality. Once in Hungary, you'll usually need to apply for a residence permit as a student. Consult with the Hungarian embassy in the country of your origin or consulate for specific visa requirements.
- Letter of acceptance. This document is issued by the Hungarian university or institution where you have been accepted. It confirms your enrollment and program details.
- You may need to demonstrate that you have sufficient funds to cover your tuition fees and living expenses in Hungary. This can include bank statements, scholarship award letters, or financial sponsorship documents.
- You'll likely need to provide proof of valid health insurance coverage in Hungary. Some universities may require you to purchase a specific health insurance plan.
- Typically, you'll need several passport-sized photos for visa and residence permit applications and student identification cards.
- Provide copies of your academic transcripts and certificates, including high school and previous degree qualifications. Some programs may have specific educational requirements.

- If your program is taught in a language other than your native language, you may need to provide language proficiency test scores, such as IELTS, TOEFL, or others, as required.
- Include a detailed CV or resume highlighting your academic achievements, work experience, and relevant extracurricular activities.
- Write a statement of purpose or motivation letter explaining why you want to study in Hungary, your academic and career goals, and how the chosen program aligns with your aspirations.
- Provide evidence of your accommodations in Hungary, such as a housing contract or confirmation of university dormitory placement.
- You may be required to submit a copy of your birth certificate as part of your application.

PR / Citizenship

If you are a citizen of another European Union (EU) or European Economic Area (EEA) country, you have the right to live and work in Hungary without needing a residence permit. However, you may choose to apply for a Registration Certificate (Európai Unió Állampolgársága Bejelentése) to document your residence in Hungary.

If you are a non-EU/EEA citizen and want to obtain permanent residency in Hungary, you typically need to follow these steps:

Long-Term Visa: Initially, you may apply for a long-term visa for a specific purpose, such as work, study, family reunification, or investment.

Temporary Residence Permit: After arriving in Hungary, you must apply for a temporary residence permit, which is typically valid for up to two years.

Continuous Residence: Maintain continuous residence in Hungary throughout the validity of your temporary residence permit.

Permanent Residence Permit: After residing in Hungary for several years (usually five years of uninterrupted legal residence), you can apply for a permanent residence permit. This permit allows you to stay in Hungary indefinitely.

Job Opportunities

High-paying job opportunities in Hungary can be found in various industries and sectors. The income level largely depends on your qualifications, experience, and the specific job you pursue.

Engineering:

Hungary has a strong engineering sector, especially in the automotive and manufacturing industries. Engineers, including mechanical, electrical, and software engineers, are well-compensated for their expertise.

Medical and Healthcare:

Healthcare professionals, especially doctors and specialized medical practitioners, can earn competitive salaries in Hungary. Medical doctors often have the opportunity to work in both public and private healthcare facilities.

Pharmaceuticals and Life Sciences:

Hungary has a strong pharmaceutical industry, and pharmaceutical research, development, and production professionals can find well-paying positions.

Real Estate and Property Management:

Real estate agents, property managers, and real estate developers can earn significant income in Hungary, particularly in the urban centers where the real estate market is active.

Consulting:

Management, IT, and other specialized consultants can have lucrative careers in Hungary, providing expertise to businesses and organizations.

It's important to note that salary levels can vary depending on your qualifications, experience, the location within Hungary, and the specific employer. Additionally, Hungary offers a lower cost of living than many Western European countries, which can make high salaries go further in purchasing power.

Chapter 21:
Study Abroad Checklist for China

Studying abroad in China can offer numerous benefits, both academically and personally. China has a rich and diverse cultural heritage, and studying there provides a unique opportunity to immerse yourself in Chinese culture, language, traditions, and history. This cultural exposure can be invaluable for personal growth and global awareness.

Learning Mandarin Chinese, one of the world's most widely spoken languages can significantly enhance your language skills and career prospects. Fluency in Mandarin is an asset in many fields, especially as China's global influence grows.

China has also made significant investments in its higher education system, with several universities consistently ranking among the top in the world. Many universities offer English-taught programs, making themselves accessible to international students.

Compared to Western countries, China often offers more affordable tuition fees and lower living costs, making it an attractive destination for students looking for cost-effective education.

China is increasingly becoming a hub for research and innovation, especially in technology, engineering, and science. Students can benefit from cutting-edge research facilities and collaborations with international experts.

Additionally, China's growing economy offers numerous internship and job opportunities, particularly for students with Mandarin language skills. Companies often seek internationally educated graduates with a global perspective.

Top Ten Universities

1. Peking University (PKU)

Located in Beijing, Peking University is one of China's oldest and most prestigious institutions. It's known for its strong programs in various fields, including humanities, sciences, and social sciences.

2. Tsinghua University

Also situated in Beijing, Tsinghua University is renowned for its engineering, computer science, and technology programs. It consistently ranks among the top universities globally.

3. Fudan University

Located in Shanghai, Fudan University is known for its excellence in social sciences, business, and economics. It has a strong international reputation.

4. Zhejiang University

Zhejiang University, based in Hangzhou, is recognized for its research in science and engineering. It's part of China's "Double First Class" initiative, aiming to make it a world-class institution.

5. Shanghai Jiao Tong University (SJTU)

SJTU, also in Shanghai, is well-regarded for its engineering and business programs. It's home to the highly respected Shanghai Ranking, which ranks top universities worldwide.

6. University of Science and Technology of China (USTC)

USTC, located in Hefei, is a top research university focusing on science and technology. It's known for its contributions to the nation's scientific advancements.

7. Nanjing University

Nanjing University, situated in Nanjing, is a comprehensive institution known for its strengths in the humanities, natural sciences, and social sciences.

8. Sun Yat-sen University

Sun Yat-sen University is located in Guangzhou, known for its medical and business schools. It's a key player in China's educational landscape.

9. Harbin Institute of Technology (HIT)

HIT, located in Harbin, is renowned for its engineering and technical programs. It has a strong reputation for producing skilled engineers and innovators.

10. Wuhan University

Wuhan University, based in Wuhan, is known for its strengths in various disciplines, including medicine, engineering, and the humanities. It's one of China's oldest and most prestigious institutions.

Entry Requirements

1. Language Proficiency:

For programs taught in Chinese (Mandarin), you will typically need to demonstrate proficiency in the language. This is usually done through the HSK (Hanyu Shuiping Kaoshi) examination, which assesses your Chinese language skills. Different programs and universities may have varying HSK score requirements, so it's essential to check the specific requirements of your chosen program.

2. Academic Qualifications:

For undergraduate programs, you must provide your high school diploma or equivalent. The specific requirements for your high school qualifications may vary depending on the university and program.

You will typically need a bachelor's degree or equivalent for postgraduate programs. The degree should be relevant to the field of study you wish to pursue.

3. Entrance Examinations:

Some universities and programs may require additional entrance examinations, especially for competitive programs or if you're seeking scholarships. These exams may include subject-specific tests or interviews.

Selecting the Right Program

Determine your academic and career goals. What field of study are you interested in? Do you want to pursue undergraduate or postgraduate studies? Are you looking for research opportunities or professional development?

Decide whether you prefer studying in English or Mandarin. This choice will narrow your options as some programs are taught entirely in English, while others require proficiency in Mandarin.

Look for universities in China that offer programs in your field of interest. You can start with the list of top Chinese universities and consider other reputable institutions that may align with your goals.

Ensure that the relevant Chinese authorities accredit the universities and programs you're considering. Accreditation is a mark of quality assurance.

Review the program details on the university's website, including course curriculum, faculty, research opportunities, and any special features of the program. This will help determine if the program aligns with your interests and goals.

Think about where in China you'd like to study. China is a vast country with diverse regions, each offering a unique cultural and lifestyle experience. Consider factors like climate, urban vs. rural settings, and proximity to major cities.

Check the admission requirements for your chosen program. Ensure that you meet the academic and language proficiency prerequisites. Some programs may also require standardized tests like the GRE or GMAT.

Calculate the total cost of studying in China, including tuition fees, living expenses, and miscellaneous charges. Research scholarships and financial aid options to help cover these expenses.

Top Ten Scholarships

1. Chinese Government Scholarship (CSC)

The Chinese Government Scholarship is one of the most prestigious scholarships for international students. It covers tuition, accommodation, and provides a monthly stipend. It's available for undergraduate, master's, and doctoral students.

2. Confucius Institute Scholarship

Sponsored by Hanban (the Office of Chinese Language Council International), the Confucius Institute Scholarship supports international students studying Chinese language and culture. It includes tuition, accommodation, and a living allowance.

3. Chinese University Scholarships

Many Chinese universities offer scholarships to attract international students. These scholarships vary in eligibility criteria, coverage, and application procedures. It's advisable to check with specific universities for details.

4. Silk Road Scholarship

Initiated by China's Ministry of Education, the Silk Road Scholarship aims to promote educational cooperation and exchange along the Silk Road countries. It supports students pursuing degrees in subjects related to the Belt and Road Initiative.

5. Great Wall Program (MUST Scholarship)

The MOFCOM (Ministry of Commerce) Scholarship, also known as the Great Wall Program, supports students from developing countries pursuing a master's degree in economics, management, and other related fields.

6. Jiangsu Jasmine Scholarship

The Jiangsu Provincial Government offers this scholarship and supports international students at all levels of study. It provides full or partial tuition coverage, along with a living allowance.

7. Shanghai Government Scholarship

Sponsored by the Shanghai Municipal Government, this scholarship supports international students studying in Shanghai. It covers tuition and provides a monthly stipend.

8. Zhejiang University Scholarship

Zhejiang University offers various scholarships for international students, including the Zhejiang University Scholarship for Outstanding International Students. These scholarships cover tuition and provide a living allowance.

9. Beijing Government Scholarship

The Beijing Government Scholarship is available for international students pursuing degree programs in Beijing. It covers tuition fees, accommodation, and a monthly living allowance.

10. Tianjin Government Scholarship

The Tianjin Government Scholarship is designed to support international students studying in Tianjin. It covers tuition and provides a monthly living allowance.

Documentation

Application Form:

You must complete the university's application form, usually available on their official website. Some universities may offer online application systems.

Academic Records:

For Undergraduate Programs: High school transcripts or academic records. These should include details of your courses, grades, and graduation date.

For Postgraduate Programs: Bachelor's degree transcripts and certificates. If you have a master's degree, you may also need to provide transcripts and certificates for that level of study.

Language Proficiency Test Scores:

If you're applying for a program taught in Mandarin Chinese, you may need to provide HSK (Hanyu Shuiping Kaoshi) scores to demonstrate your Chinese language proficiency.

If you're applying for a program taught in English, you may need to provide English language proficiency test scores, such as IELTS or TOEFL.

A Letter of Recommendation:

Typically, you will need to provide one letter of recommendation (or more) from teachers, professors, or other professionals who can speak to your academic abilities and potential.

Statement of Purpose (SOP) or Personal Statement:

You will need a written statement explaining your academic and career goals, why you are interested in the program, and how it aligns with your aspirations.

Passport Copy:

Ensure you provide a clear copy of your passport's biographical page, displaying your details and photograph. Also, ensure your passport remains valid throughout your intended stay in China.

Health Examination Report:

Many Chinese universities require international students to undergo a medical examination in their home country and submit the health examination report as part of the application. This is to ensure you are in good health before arriving in China.

Financial Documents:

Proof of your ability to cover the costs of your education and living expenses in China. This may include bank statements, scholarship awards, or financial guarantee letters.

PR / Citizenship

1. Chinese Citizenship:

Obtaining Chinese citizenship is generally challenging for foreign nationals. China has strict rules on dual citizenship, and becoming a Chinese citizen means you must renounce your other citizenship. Here are some common pathways to Chinese citizenship:

Marriage to a Chinese Citizen: If you are married to a Chinese citizen and have lived in China for a specified period (usually at least five years), you may be eligible to apply for Chinese citizenship. The requirements and procedures can vary depending on the local authorities.

Birthright: Children born in China to at least one Chinese parent, are typically considered Chinese citizens. This rule applies regardless of the nationality of the other parent.

Naturalization: In some cases, China may allow foreign nationals to apply for naturalization as Chinese citizens. However, this process is often complex, and applicants are subject to stringent requirements, including a substantial residency period and contributions to China.

2. Permanent Residency (PR) in China:

Obtaining permanent residency in China, known as a "Chinese Green Card," is a more feasible option for foreign nationals than citizenship. Here are the general eligibility criteria and application process for PR:

Eligibility Criteria: Eligibility criteria for PR in China include having a stable source of income or employment, significant contributions to China, and meeting specific requirements set by the Public Security Bureau (PSB).

Application Documents: The documents required for a PR application typically include a valid passport, a residence permit, health examination reports, a criminal record check, proof of income or assets, and other supporting documents.

Application Procedure: The application process usually involves submitting your PR application to the local PSB or the Entry and Exit Administration of the Public Security Bureau. After submission, you may undergo an interview or investigation process.

Decision: The PSB will review your application, and if approved, you will be issued a Chinese Green Card, allowing you to live and work in China without needing a work or residence permit.

Job Opportunities

China offers a range of high-paying job opportunities across various industries, and the specific salaries can vary widely depending on factors such as your qualifications, experience, location, and the sector you choose

Tech Industry

China's technology sector, including companies like Alibaba, Tencent, Huawei, and ByteDance, offers high-paying positions in software development, artificial intelligence, data science, and cybersecurity. Senior software engineers, data scientists, and AI researchers often earn competitive salaries.

Finance and Banking

Cities like Shanghai and Hong Kong are major financial centers in Asia. Investment banking, finance management, risk analysis, and financial consulting positions can be highly lucrative. Roles like investment banker, financial analyst, and risk manager often command high salaries.

Management Consulting

International consulting firms like McKinsey, BCG, and Bain & Company have a strong presence in China. Management consultants, strategy consultants, and business analysts often earn high salaries due to the demand for their expertise in various industries.

Pharmaceutical and Healthcare

China's healthcare and pharmaceutical sectors are proliferating. High-paying positions include pharmaceutical researchers, medical specialists, healthcare administrators, and pharmaceutical sales representatives.

Manufacturing and Engineering

China has a significant manufacturing sector, and engineers with expertise in mechanical engineering, electrical engineering, and manufacturing processes can find high-paying positions in multinational corporations.

Energy and Renewable Resources

Positions in the energy sector, including roles related to renewable energy and sustainability, can offer high salaries. China is investing heavily in renewable energy projects.

Entertainment and Media

China's entertainment and media industries are overgrowing, with high-paying roles in film production, talent management, digital marketing, and media production.

It's important to note that salaries vary significantly based on your qualifications and experience. Additionally, the cost of living in major cities like Beijing, Shanghai, and Shenzhen can be relatively high so that salary levels are adjusted accordingly.

Chapter 22:
Study Abroad Checklist for Ireland

Ireland is known for its excellent education system. It is home to several prestigious universities and colleges that offer world-class education and are recognized globally. Also, if English is not your first language, studying in an English-speaking country like Ireland can significantly improve your language skills, which can be valuable for your future career.

Living and studying in Ireland allows you to immerse yourself in Irish culture. You'll have the opportunity to interact with locals, learn about their traditions, and explore the rich history and heritage of the country.

You will also be met with breathtaking landscapes, from lush green countryside to rugged coastlines. You can explore the beauty of the Emerald Isle during your free time and weekends. Ireland is a popular destination for international students, so you'll have the chance to meet people worldwide, build a global network of friends and contacts, and learn about one of the ancient belief systems.

This vibrant country has a strong economy, and many international students can work part-time during their studies and full-time during certain breaks. This can help you gain work experience and support your finances.

Ireland offers attractive post-study work opportunities through schemes like the "Third Level Graduate Scheme," which allows graduates to work in Ireland for a specified period after completing their studies.

Top 10 Universities

Trinity College Dublin (TCD)

Trinity College Dublin is one of Ireland's oldest and most prestigious universities. It is renowned for its academic excellence and historic campus in the heart of Dublin. TCD consistently ranks among the top universities globally.

University College Dublin (UCD)

UCD is Ireland's largest university, known for its strong emphasis on research and innovation. It offers a wide range of programs across various disciplines and has a diverse and vibrant campus community.

University College Cork (UCC)

Located in Cork, UCC is a research-intensive institution known for its strong focus on science, technology, and healthcare programs. It is also known for its beautiful campus and strong commitment to sustainability.

National University of Ireland, Galway (NUIG)

NUIG is situated in the picturesque city of Galway on the west coast of Ireland. It is known for its research excellence, particularly in medicine, science, and technology.

Dublin City University (DCU)

DCU is a young and dynamic university located in Dublin. It is recognized for its innovative teaching methods and strong links with industry, fostering a culture of entrepreneurship among its students.

University of Limerick (UL)

UL is known for its modern campus and strong emphasis on cooperative education, providing students with valuable work experience. It excels in engineering, business, and related fields.

Maynooth University

Located just outside Dublin, Maynooth University offers a wide range of programs and is known for its strong focus on humanities and social sciences. It has a vibrant campus and a close-knit community.

Dublin Institute of Technology (DIT)

DIT is now part of Technological University Dublin (TU Dublin). It is known for its prominent programs in engineering, architecture, business, and the creative arts, and it plays a significant role in Dublin's education landscape.

University of Dublin, Royal College of Surgeons in Ireland (RCSI)

RCSI is a specialized medical university located in Dublin. It is recognized internationally for its medical and healthcare programs, including surgery and pharmacy.

Dublin Business School (DBS)

DBS is a leading institution for business and management studies in Ireland. It offers a wide range of undergraduate and postgraduate business programs and has a strong reputation for employability.

Entry Requirements

The specific criteria and entry requirements for universities in Ireland can vary depending on the university, the program of study, and your individual circumstances. However, there are some standard requirements and criteria you should be aware of when applying to Irish universities:

Academic Qualifications:

You'll typically need a high school diploma or its equivalent to apply for undergraduate programs.

It would help if you generally had a relevant bachelor's degree or equivalent qualification for postgraduate programs.

English Language Proficiency:

If your primary language is not English, you will likely need to demonstrate your English language proficiency through standardized tests such as the IELTS or TOEFL. Each university may have its minimum score requirements, so check with the specific institution you're interested in.

Program-Specific Requirements:

Some programs, especially at the postgraduate level, may have additional requirements such as a strong academic background in a specific subject, relevant work experience, or submitting a portfolio for creative arts programs.

Entrance Examinations:

Some programs, particularly in medicine and dentistry, may require you to take additional entrance exams like the HPAT (Health Professions Admission Test) or GAMSAT (Graduate Medical School Admissions Test).

Reference Letters and Personal Statements:

Many universities will require you to submit reference letters from teachers or professors and a personal statement explaining your motivations and goals for pursuing the program.

Visa Requirements:

International students coming to Irelands from outside the EU/EEA may need to apply for a student visa to study in Ireland. Visa requirements and application processes can vary, so you must check the requirements on the Irish government's official website or through the Irish embassy or consulate in your home country.

Financial Proof:

You may be required to demonstrate that you have sufficient funds to cover your tuition fees and living expenses while studying in Ireland. This is often a requirement for the student visa application.

It's important to note that entry requirements can vary significantly from one university to another and even among different programs within the same university. Therefore, it's essential to carefully review the admission requirements and criteria provided by the specific university and program you are interested in.

Scholarships and Funding

Government of Ireland Scholarships for International Students

These scholarships are funded by the Irish government and support high-achieving students from non-EU/EEA countries pursuing postgraduate (master's and PhD's) studies in Ireland. The scholarships cover tuition fees, a stipend, and other allowances.

Irish Research Council Scholarships

The Irish Research Council offers a range of scholarships and fellowships for postgraduate research in various fields. These awards support Irish and international students pursuing research degrees at eligible institutions in Ireland.

Trinity College Dublin Scholarships

Trinity College Dublin offers a variety of scholarships, including the Global Excellence Undergraduate and Postgraduate Scholarships for international students. These scholarships are merit-based and provide financial support to outstanding students.

University College Dublin (UCD) Global Excellence Scholarships

UCD offers the Global Excellence Scholarship to high-achieving international students applying for full-time undergraduate or postgraduate programs. The scholarship covers a portion of tuition fees.

University College Cork (UCC) Scholarships

UCC provides scholarships for international students at both undergraduate and postgraduate levels. These scholarships are typically awarded based on academic excellence or specific criteria related to the program of study.

Government of Ireland International Education Scholarships

The Irish higher education institutions administer these scholarships, targeting non-EU/EEA students enrolled in undergraduate and postgraduate programs in Ireland. These awards cover a portion of the tuition fees.

These scholarships are aimed at non-EU/EEA students pursuing undergraduate and postgraduate studies in Ireland. The awards cover a portion of tuition fees and are administered by the Irish higher education institutions.

Maynooth University Scholarships

Maynooth University offers a range of scholarships for international students, including the Maynooth University International Scholarship for undergraduate and postgraduate students based on academic merit.

Dublin City University (DCU) Scholarships

DCU provides various scholarships for international students, including the DCU International Student Scholarships and the DCU Academic Merit Scholarships, which are awarded only to high-achieving students.

University of Limerick Scholarships

The University of Limerick offers a selection of scholarships for both undergraduate and postgraduate students. These scholarships may be based on academic excellence, leadership, or other criteria.

Fulbright Awards

The Fulbright Commission in Ireland offers a range of awards for U.S. citizens to study, research, or teach in Ireland and for Irish citizens to do the same in the United States. These awards promote cultural exchange and academic collaboration.

Required Documents

When applying to study in Ireland as an international student, you will typically need to provide a set of documents to support your application. These documents may vary slightly depending on the university or college you are applying to and the specific program you intend to pursue.

Application Form:

Complete the university's or college's application form, typically available online.

Academic Transcripts:

Provide official transcripts from your previous educational institutions, including high school (for undergraduates) or last university degrees (for postgraduate applicants). These transcripts should list your grades and courses completed.

Proof of English Proficiency:

If applicable, include standardized test scores, such as IELTS or TOEFL, to demonstrate your English language proficiency. Some universities may have specific English language requirements, so check their guidelines.

Curriculum Vitae (CV) or Resume:

Submit a CV or resume detailing your educational background, work experience, extracurricular activities, and relevant achievements.

Personal Statement or Statement of Purpose:

Write a personal statement explaining your motivations for studying in Ireland, your academic and career goals, and why you are interested in the program you are applying for.

Letters of Recommendation:

Provide reference letters from teachers, professors, or employers who can speak to your qualifications, character, and potential for success in your chosen program.

Passport Copy:

Include a copy of your passport, which should be valid for the entire duration of your studies in Ireland.

Proof of Funding:

Demonstrate that you have sufficient funds to cover your tuition fees and living expenses in Ireland. This may include bank statements, scholarship award letters, or financial guarantee documents.

Visa Documentation:

If required, prepare and submit documents for your student visa application. This may include the visa application form, proof of payment of visa fees, and other required documents, such as a police clearance certificate.

Application Fee:

Pay the required application fee as specified by the university or college.

PR / Citizenship

Post-Study Work Visas:

Graduate Route: In 2021, Ireland introduced the "Graduate Route," a new post-study work visa. Under this scheme, international students who have completed a degree at the undergraduate level or above in Ireland can stay and work in Ireland for up to 24 months after graduation.

Doctorate Extension Scheme: PhD students can extend their stay in Ireland for up to 24 months after completing their doctoral studies to seek employment or start a business.

General Work Visas:

After completing your post-study work visa, you can apply for a general employment permit, allowing you to work in Ireland. Securing employment and work experience can be a pathway to permanent residency.

Critical Skills Employment Permit:

If you find a job in Ireland that falls under the Critical Skills Occupations list and meets the relevant criteria, you can apply for a Critical Skills Employment Permit. Holders of this permit can apply for PR after two years of employment in Ireland.

Stamp 4 Permission:

After you have lived in Ireland for five years on various immigration permissions, including student and work visas, you may be eligible to apply for Stamp 4 permission, allowing you to live and work in Ireland without restrictions.

Permanent Residency (PR):

After holding a Stamp 4 permission for five years, you can apply for PR in Ireland. PR allows you to live and work in Ireland indefinitely and is a significant step toward citizenship.

Irish Citizenship:

After living in Ireland with PR for five years (which includes the years spent on other eligible visas), you may be eligible to apply for Irish citizenship. Citizenship grants you all the rights and responsibilities of an Irish citizen, including the ability to vote and work without restrictions in any EU country.

Job Opportunities

Ireland's job market has been growing steadily, and the country offers a range of job opportunities in various sectors. You can earn a high salary in Ireland by working in industries like technology, healthcare, finance, engineering, and pharmaceuticals.

Healthcare and Medicine:

Healthcare professionals such as doctors, specialists, surgeons, and nurses are in demand. Consultants and specialists in radiology and anesthesiology tend to earn high salaries.

Finance and Banking:,

Dublin is a major financial center with numerous international banks and financial institutions. High-paying jobs in this sector include investment banking, asset management, financial analysis, and risk management.

Engineering:

Engineers in various disciplines, including civil, mechanical, electrical, and software engineering, are in demand. The engineering sector in Ireland offers competitive salaries, especially for experienced professionals.

Pharmaceutical and Life Sciences:

Ireland is home to many pharmaceutical and biotechnology companies. Jobs in research and development, quality control, regulatory affairs, and manufacturing can offer high salaries.

Legal and Law:

Lawyers and legal professionals, especially those with expertise in corporate law, intellectual property, and international law, can command high salaries in Ireland.

Consulting:

Management consultants, strategy consultants, and business analysts often earn well in Ireland as they work with numerous industries to improve their operations and strategies.

Aviation and Aerospace:

Ireland has a growing aviation and aerospace sector, and jobs in this industry, such as aircraft maintenance engineers and aerospace engineers, can be lucrative.

Data Science and Analytics:

With the increasing importance of data-driven decision-making, data scientists, data analysts, and business intelligence professionals are in demand, and these roles can offer competitive salaries.

Sales and Marketing:

Sales directors, marketing managers, and business development professionals can earn high salaries, especially in technology and pharmaceutical companies.

It's important to note that salary levels can vary depending on location (e.g., Dublin generally has higher salaries), years of experience, qualifications, and the specific company or organization. Additionally, the cost of living in Ireland, particularly in major cities like Dublin, can be relatively high, so salary levels often reflect this.

Chapter 23:

Study Abroad Checklist for New Zealand

Studying abroad in New Zealand offers a multitude of benefits that make it an attractive destination for international students. One of the foremost advantages is the high-quality education system. New Zealand is home to several world-renowned universities and institutions that consistently rank well globally. These institutions offer a wide range of programs and courses, ensuring students can find a suitable academic path.

New Zealand is known for its welcoming and inclusive society. International students often find themselves in a multicultural environment that fosters cross-cultural understanding and global perspectives. This exposure to diverse cultures enhances interpersonal and intercultural skills, which are increasingly valuable in our interconnected world.

Another significant benefit of studying here is the country's natural beauty and outdoor recreational opportunities. The stunning landscapes, from snow-capped mountains to pristine beaches, allow students to explore and appreciate the great outdoors. Adventure enthusiasts can indulge in activities like hiking, skiing, and water sports.

New Zealand also strongly emphasizes research and innovation, making it an ideal destination for students pursuing degrees in science, technology, engineering, and mathematics (STEM) fields. The country has a vibrant research community and invests heavily in cutting-edge research facilities, making it an attractive option for those seeking academic and research excellence.

The New Zealand government also offers various scholarships and financial aid options for international students, making education more accessible and affordable. The cost of living is also relatively reasonable compared to many other English-speaking countries.

Regarding post-graduation opportunities, New Zealand provides a favorable environment for international students seeking work experience. After completing their studies, graduates can apply for post-study work visas, which allow them to work in New Zealand for a specified period. This practical experience can be invaluable for building a successful career.

Top 10 Universities in New Zealand

University of Auckland

The University of Auckland is New Zealand's largest and most prestigious university, consistently ranked among the top 100 universities globally. It offers many academic programs and claims an exceptional research-oriented environment.

University of Otago

Located in Dunedin, the University of Otago is renowned for its excellence in research and teaching, particularly in health sciences, humanities, and natural sciences. It has a rich history and an outstanding reputation.

University of Canterbury

Known for its picturesque campus in Christchurch, the University of Canterbury excels in engineering, science, and technology disciplines. It's a hub for innovation and research in New Zealand.

Victoria University of Wellington

Victoria University of Wellington is in the capital city and is esteemed for its social sciences, humanities, and business programs. It offers a vibrant and diverse academic environment.

University of Waikato

Located in Hamilton, the University of Waikato is known for its strong focus on research and innovation, especially in fields like agriculture, environmental science, and computer science.

Massey University

Massey University is New Zealand's leading institution for agriculture, veterinary science, and related disciplines. It has multiple campuses across the country, offering a diverse range of programs.

Lincoln University

Lincoln University is a top choice for those interested in the agri-food sector, specializing in agriculture, agribusiness, and related fields. It has a strong emphasis on sustainability and environmental science.

AUT University (Auckland University of Technology)

AUT is known for its modern approach to education, focusing on practical and industry-relevant programs. It's a popular choice for students pursuing careers in business, technology, and creative arts.

University of Waikato

Located in Hamilton, the University of Waikato is known for its strong focus on research and innovation, especially in fields like agriculture, environmental science, and computer science.

University of Otago

The University of Otago, situated in Dunedin, is renowned for its excellence in research and teaching. It particularly shines in health sciences, humanities, and natural sciences. With a rich history dating back to 1869, this university has a strong international reputation and offers a wide range of academic programs. Its beautiful campus and commitment to academic excellence make it a top choice for students seeking a well-rounded education in New Zealand.

Entry Requirements

University entry requirements in New Zealand can vary depending on the specific institution and program you are interested in. However, some general guidelines and standard requirements apply to most universities.

Academic Qualifications:

High School Diploma: For undergraduate programs, international students must have completed their secondary education, equivalent to New Zealand's National Certificate of Educational Achievement (NCEA) Level 3 or another recognized qualification.

Bachelor's Degree: For admission to postgraduate programs, you must have completed a relevant bachelor's degree or equivalent. Some programs may require a specific minimum GPA or academic standing.

English Language Proficiency:

English Proficiency Test: Most universities require international students to demonstrate their English language proficiency. Commonly accepted tests include IELTS, TOEFL, or PTE Academic. The required scores can vary but generally fall in the IELTS 6.0-7.0 range, TOEFL iBT 80-100, or PTE Academic 58-65 for undergraduate programs, and higher scores for postgraduate programs.

Waivers: Some universities may waive the English language requirement if your previous education was conducted in English or if you can provide evidence of sufficient proficiency through other means.

Finding the Right Program

Finding the right program in New Zealand involves a thoughtful and systematic approach to ensure that your academic and career goals align with the options available.

Start by identifying your academic and career goals. What field of study are you interested in? What are your long-term career aspirations? Understanding your goals will guide your program search. New Zealand has several universities and institutions offering a wide range of programs. Research these institutions to determine which ones excel in your chosen field of study. Consider factors like reputation, location, and campus facilities.

Think about where you want to study in New Zealand. Each city or region may offer different advantages. Auckland, for instance, is the largest city and offers a wide variety of programs, while smaller cities like Dunedin or Hamilton may have a more relaxed atmosphere. Visit the websites of the universities and institutions you're interested in to explore their program offerings. Pay attention to the specific courses, curriculum, and any specializations within your field of interest.

Review the admission requirements for each program. Ensure you meet the academic prerequisites, English language proficiency requirements, and additional requirements like entrance exams or interviews. Different programs may have varying durations and structures. Determine whether you're looking for undergraduate, postgraduate, or doctoral programs and prefer a coursework-based or research-based program.

Calculate the tuition fees for your chosen program, and consider your budget. Remember that some programs offer scholarships or financial aid for international students. Explore scholarship opportunities provided by New Zealand universities, government agencies, and external organizations. Scholarships can help alleviate the financial burden of studying abroad.

Consult with academic advisors, teachers, or professors who can guide program selection based on your academic strengths and interests. They can also help you understand the relevance of your chosen program to your career goals. Reach out to alums or current students of the program or institution you're interested in. They can provide insights into the program's quality, faculty, and the overall student experience.

Think about your personal preferences and lifestyle choices. Consider the cultural and recreational opportunities in the region where you plan to study. Participate in education fairs, webinars, or information sessions organized by New Zealand universities and institutions. These events can provide valuable information and an opportunity to ask questions.

Scholarships and Funding

New Zealand Government Scholarships

The New Zealand government funds these prestigious scholarships which are available to international students at all levels of study, including undergraduate, postgraduate, and doctoral programs. They cover tuition fees, living expenses, and other costs.

Fulbright New Zealand Scholarships

These scholarships, administered by Fulbright New Zealand, support academic and cultural exchanges between New Zealand and the United States. They provide opportunities for New Zealanders to study or conduct research in the U.S. and for U.S. citizens to do the same in New Zealand.

University of Auckland Scholarships

The University of Auckland offers a wide range of scholarships for both domestic and international students. These scholarships are often merit-based and cover various fields of study and academic levels.

University of Otago Scholarships

The University of Otago provides numerous scholarships for international students pursuing undergraduate or postgraduate programs. These scholarships can assist with tuition fees and living expenses.

Victoria University of Wellington Scholarships

Victoria University of Wellington offers a variety of scholarships, including the Wellington International Excellence Scholarship, which supports high-achieving international students.

University of Canterbury Scholarships

The University of Canterbury provides several scholarships for international students, such as the UC International First Year Scholarship and UC International College Scholarships.

Massey University Scholarships

Massey University offers scholarships for international students at various levels of study. These scholarships can help cover tuition fees and other expenses.

Lincoln University Scholarships

Lincoln University provides scholarships for international students pursuing undergraduate, postgraduate, or doctoral programs concentrating on agriculture, environmental science, and related fields.

AUT Scholarships (Auckland University of Technology)

AUT offers scholarships supporting international students pursuing undergraduate and postgraduate business, health sciences, and creative arts programs.

Education New Zealand Scholarships

Education New Zealand offers a range of scholarships for international students, including the New Zealand Excellence Awards and New Zealand ASEAN Scholar Awards, designed to promote educational ties between New Zealand and specific regions.

Documentation

Start by completing the university's online or paper application forms if available. This form serves as the initial step in the application process.

Academic Transcripts:

Submit certified copies of your academic transcripts and certificates from your previous educational institutions. These documents should provide details of your academic performance and qualifications.

Proof of English Language Proficiency:

If English is not your native language, you will typically need to provide proof of English language proficiency through standardized tests such as IELTS, TOEFL, or PTE Academic. Ensure that your scores meet the specific requirements of the university and program you're applying to.

Personal Statement:

Write a statement of purpose (SOP) or personal statement explaining your academic and career goals, why you want to study in New Zealand, and your interest in the specific program.

Passport Copy:

Provide a certified copy of your passport, including your personal information, photograph, and passport number. Ensure that your passport is valid for your intended stay in New Zealand.

Proof of Funds:

Demonstrate your ability to cover tuition fees and living expenses in New Zealand. This may include bank statements, financial guarantee letters, or scholarship award letters.

Visa and Immigration Documents:

Be prepared to provide documents related to your visa application, including visa application forms, health and character certificates, and any other documents required by the New Zealand Immigration Service.

Application Fee:

Many universities in New Zealand charge an application fee. Ensure that you pay this fee as part of your application process. Keep copies of payment receipts as proof.

Translations and Notarization:

You may need to provide certified translations if your documents are not in English. Additionally, some universities may require notarized copies of your documents.

PR/Citizenship

New Zealand offers several pathways for international students to pursue permanent residency (PR) or citizenship after graduation.

1. Post-Study Work Visa (Open):

After completing your studies in New Zealand, you may be eligible for a Post-Study Work Visa (Open). This visa allows you to stay and work in New Zealand for up to 12 months. During this time, you can explore job opportunities related to your field of study, which could lead to long-term employment.

2. Post-Study Employer-Assisted Work Visa:

If you find a job related to your qualifications and your employer is willing to support your visa application, you can apply for a Post-Study Employer-Assisted Work Visa. This visa is typically granted for up to 2 or 3 years and provides a pathway to gaining valuable work experience.

3. Skilled Migrant Category (SMC) Visa:

New Zealand's Skilled Migrant Category is a points-based system that considers your age, work experience, qualifications, and job offer. If you meet the required points threshold, you can apply for this visa, which may lead to permanent residency.

4. Long Term Skill Shortage List (LTSSL) Work Visa:

If your occupation is on the LTSSL and you have a job offer in that field, you may be eligible for a work visa. Gaining work experience on this visa can contribute to your eligibility for permanent residency.

5. Residence from Work Visa:

After working in New Zealand on a work visa for a specified period, you may be eligible to apply for a Residence from Work Visa. This can ultimately lead to permanent residency if you meet the requirements.

6. Partner or Family Sponsorship:

If you have a New Zealand citizen, permanent resident partner, or family member, they may be able to sponsor you for a visa, which can lead to permanent residency.

7. Citizenship:

You can apply for New Zealand citizenship after obtaining permanent residency and meeting specific criteria. Citizenship provides a New Zealand citizen's full rights and benefits, including the ability to vote and live in the country indefinitely.

It's important to note that the specific requirements and eligibility criteria for these visa pathways can change over time. Therefore, it's crucial to consult the New Zealand Immigration Service (INZ) or an immigration advisor to get the most up-to-date and accurate information tailored to your individual circumstances.

Job Opportunities

Skilled Employment:

If you have completed a degree or qualification in a field that is in demand in New Zealand, you may be eligible for skilled employment. Jobs in engineering, healthcare, information technology, agriculture, and education are often in demand. Skilled workers can apply for work visas or permanent residency.

Post-Study Work Opportunities:

New Zealand provides post-study work visas that allow international graduates to stay in the country and work for a specific duration after completing their studies. The length of the visa depends on the level of qualification obtained. This period provides graduates with valuable work experience and opportunities to explore job prospects in their chosen field.

Graduate Programs:

Some New Zealand companies offer graduate programs designed for recent graduates. These programs provide structured training and development opportunities, often leading to permanent positions within the organization. These programs are common in finance, engineering, and consulting sectors.

Research and Academia:

Graduates who have completed advanced degrees (master's or Ph.D.) may find opportunities in research and academia. Universities and research institutions in New Zealand often hire researchers and teaching assistants in various fields.

Healthcare and Nursing:

New Zealand has a growing healthcare sector, and there is a consistent demand for healthcare professionals, including doctors, nurses, and allied health workers. Many international students in healthcare-related programs find employment in this sector.

Agriculture and Farming:

Agriculture is a significant industry in New Zealand, and there are opportunities for graduates in fields like agricultural science, horticulture, and viticulture. Seasonal work is also available in fruit picking and farm labor sectors.

Tourism and Hospitality:

New Zealand's thriving tourism industry offers job opportunities in hotels, restaurants, and tourism-related businesses. Graduate degrees in hospitality management, tourism, or related fields can find work in this sector.

Information Technology (IT):

New Zealand's IT sector continues to grow, and there is a demand for IT professionals, including software developers, system administrators, and cybersecurity experts. Graduates in computer science and IT-related fields are well-placed in this industry.

Creative Industries:

Graduates with talents in the creative arts, including film, animation, design, and music, can explore opportunities in New Zealand's thriving creative industries. The film industry, in particular, has gained international recognition.

Engineering and Construction:

New Zealand has ongoing infrastructure development projects, creating opportunities for engineers, architects, and construction professionals. Graduates in civil engineering, architecture, and related fields may find employment in this sector.

Business and Finance:

The business and finance sector in New Zealand provides opportunities for graduates in fields such as finance, accounting, marketing, and management. Many multinational companies have a presence in the country.

Environmental and Sustainability Jobs:

New Zealand places a strong emphasis on environmental conservation and sustainability. Graduates with environmental science, ecology, or sustainable development degrees may find opportunities in this sector.

Researching the specific job market in your field of interest and networking with professionals in your chosen industry is essential. Utilize career services offered by your university, attend job fairs, and consider internships or part-time jobs during your studies to gain relevant experience and increase your chances of finding the right job after graduation.

Chapter 24:

Study Abroad Checklist for Japan

Studying abroad in Japan offers many benefits that make it an attractive destination for international students. First and foremost, Japan is renowned for its world-class education system, boasting some of the top universities in Asia and the world. Students have access to cutting-edge research facilities, experienced faculty, and a rigorous academic environment, which can significantly enhance their educational and career prospects.

One of the most enticing aspects of studying in Japan is the opportunity to immerse oneself in a rich and unique culture. Japan is a country steeped in tradition and history, and living there allows students to experience its customs, festivals, and daily life firsthand. This cultural immersion can broaden one's perspective and deepen one's understanding of the world, fostering tolerance and adaptability.

Japan is known for its safety and low crime rates, making it a secure environment for international students. The country's efficient public transportation system and well-maintained infrastructure also make it easy for students to explore and travel within the country, allowing them to discover its diverse landscapes, from bustling cities like Tokyo to serene rural areas.

Language acquisition is another significant advantage of studying in Japan. While many universities offer courses in English, the opportunity to learn Japanese or improve language skills is invaluable. Proficiency in Japanese can open doors to a wide range of job opportunities in Japan and internationally, particularly in industries like technology, finance, and international business.

Japan is also a global economic powerhouse, home to prominent multinational corporations and innovative startups. Studying in Japan provides students networking opportunities and access to internships, enhancing their prospects for future employment in the country or globally. The Japanese work ethic and business culture can provide valuable insights and skills highly sought after in today's global job market.

In addition to all these advantages, studying in Japan allows students to forge international friendships that can last a lifetime. The country's warm and welcoming atmosphere and rich cultural heritage make it easy for students to connect with locals and fellow international students, creating a diverse and supportive community.

Top 10 Universities

University of Tokyo (Todai):

The University of Tokyo, often referred to as Todai, is Japan's most prestigious and oldest institution. It consistently ranks among the top universities globally and offers diverse academic programs across various disciplines.

Kyoto University:

Kyoto University is renowned for its excellence in research and education. It is particularly well-regarded in fields such as science, engineering, and humanities and has a long history of producing Nobel laureates.

Osaka University:

Osaka University is known for its strong emphasis on innovation and research. It is a leader in science and technology-related disciplines and is a hub for cutting-edge research initiatives.

Tokyo Institute of Technology (Tokyo Tech):

Tokyo Tech is a top-tier institution specializing in science and engineering. It is known for its rigorous academic programs and contributions to technological advancements.

Tohoku University:

Tohoku University in Sendai is regarded for its research in various fields, including natural sciences, medicine, and engineering. It has a strong international presence and collaborative research projects.

Nagoya University:

Nagoya University is recognized for its comprehensive academic offerings and contributions to physics, chemistry, and social sciences research. It has a strong commitment to internationalization.

Kyushu University:

Kyushu University, located in Fukuoka, is known for its global outlook and research initiatives. It offers a diverse range of programs and strongly emphasizes fostering international partnerships.

Hokkaido University:

Hokkaido University, based in Sapporo, is a prominent research institution known for its excellence in agriculture, environmental science, and engineering. It promotes interdisciplinary research and global collaboration.

Keio University:

Keio University is a leading private institution with a strong focus on liberal arts education. It offers various programs, including business, law, and social sciences, and is known for its global network.

Waseda University:

Waseda University is another prestigious private university in Japan, offering programs in a variety of fields, including humanities, social sciences, and business. It has a strong emphasis on internationalization and research.

Entry Requirements

University entry requirements in Japan can vary depending on the institution, degree program, and whether you are applying as a domestic or international student. Here are some general guidelines for university entry requirements in Japan:

High School Diploma or Equivalent:

For undergraduate programs, Japanese universities typically require applicants to complete their high school education or equivalent. This is the minimum educational qualification for admission.

Language Proficiency:

If you are an international student and your chosen program is taught in Japanese, you may need to demonstrate your Japanese language proficiency. This is usually done through standardized tests like the Japanese Language Proficiency Test (JLPT) or the Japanese University Admission for International Students (EJU) Examination.

Entrance Examinations:

Entrance examinations are a significant part of the admission process in Japan. Most Japanese universities, especially prestigious ones, require applicants to take standardized entrance exams specific to the university or the department they are applying to. These exams typically include subjects related to the chosen field of study.

Academic Transcripts:

You will need to provide your high school transcripts or academic records as part of your application. These transcripts should show your academic performance during your high school years.

Finding the Right Program

If you're trying to find the right program at a university in Japan, it's essential to begin with a clear understanding of your academic and career goals. Take the time to define your passions and long-term aspirations, considering which subjects or fields resonate with you.

This self-awareness will be the foundation for selecting the program that aligns most closely with your interests and objectives.

Once you've established your goals, the next step involves thoroughly researching Japanese universities. Look for institutions that offer programs in your chosen field of study, and consider various factors such as the university's reputation, location, campus facilities, and the availability of resources related to your subject. This comprehensive exploration will help you identify universities that are a good fit for your academic pursuits.

Language of instruction is another crucial consideration. Determine whether you prefer to study in English or Japanese. Some universities offer programs taught in English to accommodate international students, while others require proficiency in Japanese. Ensuring that the language of instruction aligns with your language skills is essential for your academic success and overall experience.

Delve into the specifics of each university's program offerings. Explore the curriculum, courses, and specialization options they provide. Seek programs that match your academic interests and align with your career goals, ensuring that the coursework and focus areas align with your aspirations.

It's vital to check the admission requirements for each program you're interested in. Verify that you meet the academic prerequisites and language proficiency requirements. Be mindful of additional admission criteria, such as standardized tests, recommendation letters, or interviews, as these may vary between universities and programs.

Consider the university's location, as it will impact your overall experience. Evaluate factors like the cost of living, climate, proximity to major cities or industry hubs, and cultural attractions. A comfortable and conducive environment is essential for your well-being during your studies in Japan.

Check how much your education will cost, considering tuition, fees, and what you need for daily living. Look for scholarships, grants, and financial aid offered to students from other countries. Create a budget to determine whether the program is financially feasible for you, considering all potential expenses.

You must ensure that the university and program you're interested in are accredited and recognized. Investigate university rankings and academic reputation to gauge the quality of education you can expect.

Reach out to current or former students who have attended the university or program you're considering. They can provide invaluable insights into the academic environment, faculty, and student life, helping you make a well-informed decision.

Participate in university information sessions and education fairs in your home country or online. These events offer opportunities to interact with university representatives and gather detailed information about the programs and admission procedures.

Finally, seek guidance from academic advisors or counselors who can provide expert advice on program selection, application processes, and available scholarships. Their experience and expertise can be instrumental in navigating the complexities of choosing the right program at a Japanese university, setting you on a path to a fulfilling educational experience.

Scholarships

Japanese Government (MEXT) Scholarships:

The Japanese Government (MEXT) Scholarships are among the most prestigious scholarships for international students. They are offered at various levels, including undergraduate, graduate, and research programs. MEXT Scholarships cover tuition, living expenses, and round-trip airfare.

JASSO Scholarships (Monbukagakusho Honors Scholarship for Privately-Financed International Students):

The Japan Student Services Organization (JASSO) provides scholarships to privately financed international students based on academic achievement. These scholarships help cover tuition fees and living expenses.

Asian Development Bank-Japan Scholarship Program:

Administered by the Asian Development Bank (ADB), this scholarship program offers financial support to students from ADB member countries pursuing postgraduate studies in Japan. It covers tuition, living expenses, and other educational costs.

Rotary Peace Fellowships:

The Rotary Peace Fellowships are for individuals pursuing a master's degree or professional development certificate in peace and conflict resolution fields. Recipients receive funding for tuition, living expenses, and travel.

JSPS Postdoctoral Fellowships:

The Japan Society for the Promotion of Science (JSPS) offers postdoctoral fellowships for researchers worldwide. These fellowships support research activities at Japanese universities and research institutions.

Toyota Foundation Research Grants:

The Toyota Foundation provides research grants to support projects contributing to societal and cultural advancement in Japan and other Asian countries—these grants fund research activities and initiatives.

Yamaha Music Foundation Scholarships:

The Yamaha Music Foundation offers scholarships to outstanding music students pursuing degrees or diplomas in music-related fields in Japan. The scholarships provide financial support for tuition and living expenses.

Nitori International Scholarship Foundation:

The Nitori International Scholarship Foundation supports international students studying in Japan, including undergraduate and graduate students. Scholarships are awarded based on academic performance and financial need.

Japan-IMF Scholarship Program for Advanced Studies:

This scholarship program, sponsored by the International Monetary Fund (IMF), supports students from selected Asian countries pursuing graduate-level studies in economics or related fields in Japan.

Kobe University Graduate School Scholarships for International Students:

Kobe University offers a range of scholarships for international students pursuing graduate studies. These scholarships help cover tuition fees and living expenses.

Documentation

Application Form:

Most universities in Japan provide an online application form that you must complete. This form typically includes personal information, educational history, and program preferences.

Academic Transcripts:

You will need to provide official transcripts from your previous educational institutions, such as high school or undergraduate institutions. These transcripts should detail your academic performance, courses taken, and grades earned.

Diploma or Degree Certificate:

Depending on the program level you are applying to (undergraduate, graduate, or doctoral), you may need to submit a copy of your high school diploma, bachelor's degree certificate, or equivalent documentation.

Language Proficiency Test Scores:

If you are applying for a program taught in Japanese and your native language is not Japanese, you may need to provide language proficiency test scores. The most commonly accepted tests are the Japanese Language Proficiency Test (JLPT) and the Japanese University Admission for International Students (EJU) Examination. If applying for an English-taught program, you may need to provide scores for tests like TOEFL or IELTS.

Standardized Test Scores:

Some universities may require standardized test scores, such as the SAT or ACT for undergraduate programs or the GRE or GMAT for graduate programs. Check the specific program's admission requirements.

Letters of Recommendation:

Many universities request letters of recommendation from teachers, professors, or professionals who can attest to your academic abilities and character. Ensure you follow the university's guidelines regarding the number of letters required and submission procedures.

Statement of Purpose or Personal Statement:

Prepare a well-written statement of purpose or personal statement that explains your academic and career goals, why you are interested in the program, and how it aligns with your aspirations.

Passport Copy:

A copy of your passport's photo page may be required for identification purposes.

Photographs:

Some universities may request passport-sized photographs for administrative purposes. Check the university's guidelines for photo specifications.

Financial Documentation (for Visa Application):

To obtain a student visa, you will need to provide proof of sufficient funds to cover your tuition fees and living expenses in

Japan. This may include bank statements, scholarship award letters, or financial affidavits.

PR / Citizenship

1. Post-Study Work Visa (Designated Activities Visa):

After completing your studies in Japan, you can apply for a post-study work visa, officially known as the Designated Activities Visa. This visa allows you to stay in Japan for up to one year to search for employment or engage in job-hunting activities. You can transition to a work visa if you secure a job during this period.

2. Work Visas:

Once you find employment in Japan, you can switch to a work visa, depending on your job type.

The work visa categories include Engineer/Specialist in Humanities/International Services, Instructor, Skilled Labor, and more. These visas are typically granted for specific job roles and are a common pathway for long-term stay in Japan.

3. Highly Skilled Professional Visa:

Japan offers a Highly Skilled Professional (HSP) Visa designed to attract and retain highly skilled foreign professionals. The HSP visa has different categories, each with its own point system. Points are awarded based on education, work experience, and annual income. Achieving a certain point threshold can lead to preferential immigration treatment, including a shorter PR application waiting period.

4. Permanent Residency (PR):

To become a permanent resident in Japan, you must meet specific requirements, such as residing in Japan for a certain number of years (usually ten years). However, individuals with an HSP visa may be eligible for PR in as few as one year of residence. PR allows you to live and work in Japan indefinitely, with no restrictions on employment or location.

5. Naturalization (Citizenship):

Gaining Japanese citizenship through naturalization is possible but challenging. To be eligible, you generally need to have lived in Japan for at least five years, demonstrate good conduct, be financially stable, and be willing to renounce your previous citizenship(s), as Japan does not allow dual citizenship. Additionally, you must pass a Japanese language proficiency test and an interview.

It's important to note that Japan has strict immigration policies and requirements. Meeting the minimum stay and eligibility criteria is necessary for each stage of the immigration process. Furthermore, Japan's approach to naturalization can be quite demanding compared to other countries.

To increase your chances of obtaining a post-study work visa, PR, or citizenship in Japan, consider the following:

- Maintain an excellent academic and professional record.
- Learn the Japanese language, as proficiency is often required for PR and citizenship.
- Abide by Japanese immigration laws and regulations.
- Seek legal advice or assistance when applying for visas or PR.

Japan values skilled professionals and welcomes international talent, but it's crucial to navigate the immigration process carefully and understand the specific requirements and procedures involved in achieving your immigration goals in the country.

Job opportunities

Japan offers a wide range of job opportunities for both its citizens and international residents. The country's job market is diverse, with opportunities in various industries and sectors. Here are some of the different types of job opportunities available in Japan:

Technology and IT:

Japan is home to several global technology giants and a thriving IT sector. Technology job opportunities include software development, data analysis, network engineering, and cybersecurity. The country also has a growing startup ecosystem, providing opportunities for entrepreneurs and tech enthusiasts.

Manufacturing and Engineering:

Japan has a strong manufacturing sector known for the automotive, electronics, machinery, and robotics industries. Jobs in this sector include mechanical and electrical engineering, quality control, production management, and research and development.

Finance and Banking:

Tokyo is a major financial hub in Asia, offering a wide range of banking, finance, and investment opportunities. Roles include financial analysts, investment bankers, financial consultants, and asset managers.

Healthcare and Pharmaceuticals:

Japan's aging population has led to an increased demand for healthcare professionals. Job opportunities include doctors, nurses, pharmacists, medical researchers, and healthcare administrators.

Education and Language Teaching:

Teaching English as a foreign language is a popular job option for expatriates in Japan. The Japan Exchange and Teaching (JET) Program is one well-known initiative for English language teaching. There are also opportunities to teach other subjects at international schools and universities.

Tourism and Hospitality:

Japan's tourism industry has grown steadily, creating opportunities for hotels, restaurants, tour guides, and travel agencies. Proficiency in Japanese and English can be an advantage in this sector.

Retail and Sales:

Retail jobs are abundant in Japan, ranging from department store sales associates to marketing and management positions.

Consulting and Business Services:

Consulting firms in various fields, including management, finance, and IT, offer job opportunities for professionals with expertise in these areas.

Translation and Interpretation:

Bilingual individuals can find work as translators or interpreters, helping bridge language gaps between Japanese and non-Japanese speakers in various industries.

Creative and Entertainment:

Opportunities in the creative and entertainment industries include jobs in advertising, film and television production, graphic design, animation, and video game development.

Research and Academia:

Japan has a vital research and academic community. Positions at universities, research institutions, and think tanks are available for scholars and researchers.

Agriculture and Food Industry:

Agriculture-related jobs include farming, food production, and food safety management. Japan's culinary scene also offers chefs, cooks, and restaurant staff opportunities.

Environmental and Renewable Energy:

As sustainability gains importance, Japan focuses on environmental initiatives and renewable energy. Jobs in this sector include environmental engineers, renewable energy specialists, and sustainability consultants.

Government and Public Sector:

The Japanese government and public sector offer administration, policy analysis, diplomacy, and civil service positions. Foreign nationals may find opportunities in international organizations or diplomatic missions.

It's important to note that language proficiency, particularly in Japanese, can significantly impact your job prospects in Japan. Many professional roles require a strong command of the Japanese language, as it is the country's primary language of business and communication.

Chapter 25:
Ensuring Your Safety Abroad

Embarking on a journey to study abroad is a thrilling adventure filled with the promise of new experiences, cultures, and personal growth. However, with this excitement comes the need for careful preparation, especially when it comes to ensuring your health and safety. I will delve into the essential aspects of life abroad, offering comprehensive guidance on how to conduct yourself responsibly and confidently in unfamiliar territory. From securing your health and safety to familiarizing yourself with the legal landscape, I'll provide valuable insights and practical advice to help you maximize your study abroad experience while staying well-informed and respectful of your host country's customs and laws.

Safety

Before embarking on your journey, it's crucial to prioritize your well-being through thorough pre-departure health preparations. Consult with your healthcare provider to ensure you have all the vaccinations and prescriptions for your destination. Additionally, discuss your travel plans with them to address any specific health concerns. Investing in a comprehensive health insurance policy covering medical expenses, emergencies, and potential evacuation is wise. Always carry copies of essential documents like your passport, visa, and travel insurance, and consider digital copies stored securely in the cloud or emailed to yourself for easy access.

Research and familiarize yourself with local healthcare resources, such as hospitals, clinics, and pharmacies in your host city. Make a note of emergency contact numbers specific to your destination, which can be invaluable in urgent situations. Prepare a health and safety kit, including first aid supplies, pain relievers, antiseptic wipes, and any prescribed medications. Pack a small flashlight, pocketknife, and a portable phone charger to be ready for unexpected circumstances. Stay informed about travel vaccinations and follow local health guidelines, including food and water safety precautions.

Your travel insurance should be a comprehensive safety net, so thoroughly understand your policy's coverage. Keep a physical copy of your insurance policy and the contact information for your insurer within easy reach. Embrace cultural awareness by researching local customs, laws, and regulations. Demonstrating respect for cultural norms and avoiding offensive or illegal behaviors is essential for your safety and positive interactions with locals. Establish emergency contacts by sharing your travel itinerary and contact details with family or friends back home. Keep the contact information for your home country's embassy or consulate in your host city readily available.

Traveling in numbers is a wise choice for safety. When exploring or moving around, especially in unfamiliar areas or at night, it's advisable to be accompanied by others. Be aware of the local emergency evacuation procedures, and know the assembly points, especially in your accommodation.

Establish a communication plan with your study abroad program or university in case of emergencies. Staying informed about local news and developments is crucial, particularly in regions with political instability or natural disasters. Register with your embassy or consulate if they offer such a service, as it can aid communication and support during emergencies. Finally, trust your instincts: if you ever feel uncomfortable or unsafe, prioritize your well-being by removing yourself from it and seeking help if necessary.

Healthcare System

Firstly, research and familiarize yourself with the healthcare system of your host country. Understand whether the country provides universal healthcare or requires individuals to have private insurance. This knowledge will be essential in guiding your next steps.

For example, in Canada, healthcare is provided through a publicly funded system known as the Canada Health Act. As an international student, you may be eligible for provincial or territorial healthcare coverage, but this eligibility varies depending on the province or territory you're studying. Most provinces and territories require international students to be in Canada for at least six months with a study permit to qualify for their healthcare plan.

After meeting these requirements, you can typically apply for provincial or territorial health coverage through your institution's international student office or directly with the healthcare authority in your province. While waiting to qualify for provincial healthcare, you'll need private health insurance to cover your medical expenses. Many educational institutions offer group health insurance plans for international students, or you can purchase private insurance from providers like *Guard Me* or *Sun Life Financial*. The costs and coverage of healthcare plans differ across provinces, so it's crucial to understand the specifics of the plan in your region.

In France, healthcare is universal and primarily funded through social security contributions. International students can also access the French healthcare system, which involves social security registration. If you are between 18 and 28 years old and studying in France for more than three months, you may be eligible for French social security coverage. To obtain this coverage, you must apply through a local student social security office called "La Sécurité Sociale Étudiante" upon arriving in France. Once registered, you will receive a healthcare card, or "Carte Vitale," allowing you to access healthcare services conveniently.

While French social security covers many medical expenses, it doesn't cover everything. Therefore, many students opt for complementary health insurance, known as "mutuelle," to fill the gaps. Some popular providers include LMDE and MEP.

In the Netherlands, healthcare is mandatory for all residents, including international students. To obtain health coverage, international students must have Dutch health insurance, even if they have insurance from their home country. Dutch health insurance typically consists of basic and supplementary coverage, with the basic insurance covering essential medical care.

To get Dutch health insurance, you must register with an insurance provider and provide your Citizen Service Number (BSN), which you receive upon arriving in the Netherlands. The cost of Dutch health insurance can vary depending on the provider and the level of coverage you choose, with students often paying around €100-€120 per month for basic insurance. Supplementary insurance, such as dental care or physiotherapy, is available for additional coverage.

Next, check the specific requirements for health coverage for international students in your host country. Many countries have specific insurance requirements for international students, which is crucial to understand. These may include mandatory enrollment in a national healthcare system, purchasing a private insurance policy, or a combination of both.

Once you clearly understand the requirements, you'll need to identify the options available to you. This may include enrolling in a national healthcare program if eligible, purchasing a private health insurance policy designed for international students, or combining both to ensure comprehensive coverage.

When considering private health insurance, research and compare different insurance providers. Their coverage includes medical services, prescription medications, and emergency care. Pay attention to coverage limits, deductibles, and any additional benefits, such as dental or vision care coverage.

The enrollment process for health insurance will depend on the country and the insurance provider. You may need to fill out application forms, provide documentation such as proof of enrollment in your educational institution, and pay premiums. Be sure to understand the coverage start date, as it may be required immediately upon arrival in your host country.

Lastly, maintain regular communication with your educational institution's international office or designated contact for international students. They can often provide guidance, resources, and assistance navigating the local healthcare system and meeting insurance requirements. They can also help you understand any changes in regulations or needs during your stay.

Driver's License

Acquiring a driving license in your host country can be valuable, providing mobility and independence during your time abroad. However, the process can vary significantly from one country to another. Generally, the steps to obtain a driving license in any host country involve a combination of written exams, practical driving tests, and paperwork.

Generally, you'll typically begin by researching the local requirements for obtaining a driving license. Most countries have age restrictions, so you must confirm whether you meet the minimum age requirement. In addition to age, residency requirements often may affect your eligibility. Once you've determined your eligibility, you'll need to gather the necessary documentation, including proof of identity, proof of residence, and a valid visa or residence permit.

After meeting the documentation requirements, you'll usually need to enroll in a driving school or take mandatory driving lessons, which can vary in duration and content depending on the country.

Many host countries require applicants to pass a written theory exam covering road rules, traffic signs, and safe driving practices. Study materials and practice exams are often available to help you prepare for this written test.

Once you've passed the theory exam, you'll typically move on to the practical driving test. This involves demonstrating your driving skills under the supervision of an examiner. The test will assess your ability to operate a vehicle safely and follow traffic rules. You'll need to practice your driving skills to prepare for this examination.

In Germany, for example, obtaining a driving license involves attending a certified driving school, which includes theoretical and practical training. You must be at least 17 years old to apply for a car (Class B) license. After completing your training, you'll take a theory test at the local driver's license authority (Fahrerlaubnisbehörde) and a practical driving test.

The process can be more complex in India due to diverse regulations across states. Typically, you must be 18 years old to apply for a car (Class LMV) license. You'll need to pass a written test on traffic rules and regulations and then take a practical driving test. Many states also have a learner's license stage that precedes the full license.

In Italy, driving licenses are issued by the Motorizzazione Civile. To obtain a car (Category B) license, you must be at least 18 years old. The process involves attending a driving school, passing a theory test, and taking a practical driving test. Italy also has specific requirements for international students, including obtaining a residence certificate.

Just remember that specific requirements and procedures can change, so it's essential to check with local authorities or driving schools in your host country for the most up-to-date information on obtaining a driving license.

Local Laws

Familiarizing yourself with the local laws in your host country is essential to ensuring a smooth and enjoyable experience while studying abroad. Understanding and adhering to local regulations helps you avoid legal issues and demonstrates respect for the host country's culture and legal system. In general, acquainting yourself with local laws begins with thorough research before your departure. This research should encompass a wide range of legal aspects, including but not limited to traffic regulations, alcohol and drug laws, visa and immigration requirements, and cultural norms regarding dress codes, public behavior, and social etiquette.

Spain, for example, has specific traffic laws that may differ from those in your home country. Speed limits, parking regulations, and alcohol consumption limits while driving are strictly enforced. Familiarizing yourself with these rules can help you avoid fines and ensure your safety on the road. Additionally, it's vital to be aware of Spain's visa and immigration requirements, especially if you plan to stay for an extended period. Overstaying your visa can lead to severe consequences, including deportation.

Ireland has strict regulations regarding alcohol consumption, and public drunkenness can result in fines or arrests. It's essential to be aware that the legal drinking age is 18 and to consume alcohol responsibly. Ireland also has specific rules for driving, including driving on the left side of the road, and you'll need to familiarize yourself with these rules before getting behind the wheel.

In Japan, respecting local laws and customs is of paramount importance. Japanese society places great emphasis on etiquette and politeness. For example, removing your shoes before entering someone's home is essential, and bowing is a standard greeting. Additionally, Japan has strict drug laws, and possessing even a small amount of illegal substances can lead to severe penalties, including imprisonment.

To ensure you comply with local laws, consult official government websites, embassy resources, or your host institution's international office for guidance. These sources can provide you with up-to-date information and insights into your host country's legal and cultural norms.

Chapter 26:

Immersing Yourself in the Host Culture

Immersing yourself in a foreign culture while studying abroad is one of the most rewarding aspects of the experience. It allows you to understand the local way of life better, forge meaningful connections with people, and grow personally and academically. Here are various ways to fully embrace and immerse yourself in a foreign culture.

Learning the local language is one of the most effective ways to immerse yourself in a foreign culture. Enroll in language classes, practice with locals, and use language-learning apps and resources to become proficient. Speaking the language opens doors to authentic interactions and a deeper understanding of the culture. For example, Mandarin is the official language in China, so enrolling in language classes and practicing your Mandarin is critical. Consider language exchange programs where you can meet local Chinese students and practice language skills together.

Opt for homestays or shared housing with residents rather than staying in international student dorms. Living with locals allows you to observe daily life, customs, and traditions up close. You'll also have opportunities to practice the language and build lasting friendships.

Attend cultural events, festivals, and celebrations. These gatherings offer unique insights into local traditions, music, dance, and cuisine. Engaging in cultural activities can be a vibrant and memorable way to immerse yourself in the local way of life.

Many universities abroad have student clubs and organizations catering to various interests, from sports to arts and community service. Joining these groups helps you make friends and allows you to engage in local activities and meet like-minded individuals. For example, many Chinese universities have various student clubs and organizations. Joining clubs such as calligraphy, tai chi, or traditional Chinese music can allow you to immerse yourself in Chinese arts and culture.

Food is an integral part of any culture. Sample local dishes and explore different culinary traditions. Try street food, dine at local restaurants, and consider taking cooking classes to learn how to prepare traditional meals yourself.

Take advantage of your time abroad to explore different regions within your host country. Each region often has its own unique customs, dialects, and traditions. Traveling within the country allows you to experience this diversity firsthand. Enroll in classes or workshops that teach traditional skills or arts, such as dance, music, pottery, or martial arts. Learning these skills from local experts can provide a deeper connection to the culture.

Engage in volunteer work or community service projects. Contributing to the local community fosters a sense of belonging and allows you to interact with locals while making a positive impact. Explore the literature, films, and music of your host country. This can provide valuable insights into the culture, history, and societal values.

Embrace cultural differences with an open mind and a respectful attitude. Be willing to adapt to local customs and norms, even if they differ from your own. Showing respect for the culture will facilitate meaningful connections and enrich your experience. Keep a journal, blog, or vlog to document your journey and reflections. Sharing your experiences can help you process your immersion into the culture and provide a valuable record of your time abroad.

Remember that cultural immersion is a gradual process, and challenges are expected along the way. Be patient with yourself, embrace the learning curve, and savor every moment of your cultural exploration.

Cultural Preparation

Cross-cultural preparation is vital to any international experience, particularly when studying abroad. It involves equipping yourself with the knowledge, skills, and mindset necessary to navigate and thrive in a foreign cultural context. Cross-cultural preparation is crucial because it enhances your safety and well-being and fosters a more enriching and respectful interaction with the host country's culture and people.

Adequate cross-cultural preparation helps you anticipate and manage culture shock, which is the feeling of disorientation and discomfort that can arise when confronted with unfamiliar cultural norms and practices. Understanding what to expect can significantly reduce the impact of culture shock. Learning about cultural differences in communication styles, non-verbal cues, and social etiquette enables you to communicate more effectively and avoid misunderstandings or unintentional offenses.

Cross-cultural preparation encourages empathy and cultural sensitivity. It helps you develop an appreciation for the host culture's values, customs, and traditions, fostering respectful and harmonious interactions. Being prepared to adapt to a new cultural environment enhances your adaptability. This adaptability is valuable during your time abroad and a valuable life skill that can be applied in various contexts.

For example, cross-cultural preparation for Japan should include understanding Japanese customs, such as bowing, gift-giving, and the importance of etiquette in daily life. Japanese society places a high value on politeness and harmony, so knowing how to navigate social interactions respectfully is crucial. Learning basic Japanese phrases can also be incredibly helpful, even though many Japanese people speak English.

In India, cross-cultural preparation should encompass the diversity of the country's cultures, languages, and religions. Recognize that customs and traditions can vary significantly from one region to another. For example, the customs in North India may differ from those in South India. Understanding the importance of festivals like Diwali and Holi and how they are celebrated in various regions can enhance your experience. Additionally, awareness of the caste system and its social implications is essential for cultural sensitivity.

Similarly, cross-cultural preparation for Singapore should include understanding its multicultural society, where diverse ethnic groups coexist, including Chinese, Malay, Indian, and others. Familiarize yourself with the customs and traditions of these groups, such as Chinese New Year, Deepavali, and Hari Raya Puasa. It's also vital to be aware of Singapore's strict laws and regulations on littering, public behavior, and drug offenses, as violating them can lead to severe penalties.

In all cases, consider seeking cultural sensitivity training or workshops, which many universities or organizations offer to prepare students for cross-cultural experiences. Engaging with individuals who have lived or studied in the host country can also provide valuable insights. Finally, maintaining an open, curious, and respectful attitude toward the host culture will go a long way in facilitating positive interactions and a deeper appreciation of the cultural richness of the country you are studying in.

Studying With Disabilities

Becoming a part of the culture you're studying as a person with disabilities requires a combination of preparation, adaptability, and a positive attitude. While there may be unique challenges, immersing yourself fully in a foreign culture and having a meaningful experience is possible.

Before embarking on your study abroad journey, research the accessibility and support available in your host country. Learn about local laws regarding disability rights, accessible transportation, and accommodations. Contact your host institution or program coordinators to discuss your needs and requirements. Having a well-thought-out plan will help you navigate potential challenges more effectively.

Many universities and study abroad programs offer support services for students with disabilities. These services may include accessible housing, academic accommodations, and assistance with daily tasks. Communicate your needs to your program coordinators or the university's disability support office to ensure you receive the necessary service.

Research and connect with local disability organizations or support groups in your host country. They can provide valuable insights into the local disability community, resources, and information on accessible activities and services. Engaging with these organizations can also help you connect with locals with similar experiences.

Even if English is widely spoken in your host country, learning basic phrases in the local language can be immensely helpful. It can facilitate communication, show respect for the local culture, and make interactions with locals more enjoyable.

Engage in cultural activities and experiences like local festivals, art exhibitions, or traditional performances. Many cultural events offer accessible options for people with disabilities, such as sign language interpreters or ramps. Attending these events allows you to immerse yourself in the culture and connect with locals.

Familiarize yourself with the local transportation options and their accessibility features. Many cities worldwide have accessible public transportation systems, and taxis or rideshare services may also offer accessible vehicles. Having a reliable mode of transportation enables you to explore the country more easily.

Don't hesitate to share your experiences and feedback with your host institution or program coordinators. Advocating for accessibility and inclusivity can improve the support and accommodations available to future students with disabilities.

Build relationships with local students who share your interests or are involved in disability-related initiatives. These connections can offer valuable insights into daily life in the host country and provide a sense of belonging.

Embrace opportunities to step outside your comfort zone. Be open to trying local foods, engaging in cultural practices, and participating in local traditions. These experiences can lead to meaningful connections and a deeper understanding of the culture.

Consider documenting your study abroad experience through a blog, vlog, or social media. Sharing your journey as a person with disabilities can inspire others, raise awareness, and provide a platform for sharing information and resources.

Becoming a part of the culture you're studying as a person with disabilities may require extra planning and effort, but it can lead to a transformative and enriching experience. By seeking support, advocating for accessibility, and embracing opportunities for cultural engagement, you can fully immerse yourself in the culture and create lasting memories during your study abroad adventure.

Chapter 27:

Making the Most of Your Time Abroad

Honing Your Cross-cultural Skills

Honing your cross-cultural skills while studying abroad is a valuable endeavor that enriches your overall experience and prepares you for a globalized world.

Many universities offer cultural sensitivity training or workshops in their international programs. These sessions provide insights into various aspects of cross-cultural communication, including non-verbal cues, customs, and etiquette.

1. Language Learning: Learning the local language, even if it's just basic phrases, can significantly enhance your cross-cultural skills. It shows respect for the host culture and allows for more meaningful interactions.

2. Interact with Locals: Engage with residents whenever possible. Strike up conversations, attend local events, or participate in community activities. Building relationships with locals is one of the best ways to gain cultural insights.

3. Observe and Learn: Take time to observe the local culture's daily routines, traditions, and social norms. Pay attention to how people greet each other, how they dress, and what is considered polite behavior.

4. Stay Open-Minded: Be open to new experiences and perspectives. Avoid making judgments based on your cultural norms. Instead, try to understand why certain customs exist and appreciate the diversity of beliefs and practices.

For example, in Spain, dining often involves sharing tapas small plates of various dishes. To hone your cross-cultural skills, visit local tapas bars and engage with fellow diners. You'll discover that it's common for people to share food and socialize over a leisurely meal.

Spain is famous for its vibrant festivals and flamenco dancing. Participating in these events and watching performances exposes you to Spanish culture and provides opportunities to interact with locals who share their passion for these traditions.

Another example is Dubai. It has cultural exchange centers like the Sheikh Mohammed Centre for Cultural Understanding (SMCCU), where you can attend cultural meals, guided tours, and discussions with Emiratis. These experiences allow you to learn about Emirati customs, traditions, and values firsthand.

Dubai is a diverse city with a significant Muslim population. During Ramadan, join in the fasting experience and learn about the significance of this holy month. Sharing iftar (the evening meal to break the fast) with Emirati friends can be an enlightening cultural experience.

Russia has Matryoshka Doll Painting. You can participate in workshops where you can paint Matryoshka dolls, traditional Russian nesting dolls. This artistic activity immerses you in Russian art and offers opportunities to converse with local artisans and learn about their craftsmanship.

Experiencing a Russian banya, or sauna, is a cultural adventure. Join locals in this relaxing tradition and engage in conversations. You'll discover that the banya is not just about heat and steam but also a social gathering where people share stories and build bonds.

By actively engaging in these cultural experiences and applying the general cross-cultural tips mentioned earlier, you can enhance your skills for adapting to and thriving in diverse cultural settings. Remember that cultural immersion is a journey that requires patience, an open heart, and a willingness to embrace the unfamiliar.

Learn from your mistakes

Learning from your mistakes while studying abroad and honing your cultural skills is crucial to personal, intellectual, and artistic growth. Making errors is an inevitable part of any learning process, especially when navigating unfamiliar cultural terrain. Here's how you can effectively learn from your mistakes in the context of being abroad and developing your cross-cultural skills:

Acknowledge Mistakes Openly: Recognize that making mistakes is a natural and valuable part of learning. Avoid feeling ashamed or defensive when you make cultural missteps. Instead, approach them with an open and growth-oriented mindset.

Reflect on the Mistake: Take time to reflect on what went wrong and why. Consider the cultural context and any misinterpretations or assumptions that may have led to the mistake. Self-awareness is the first step in the learning process.

Seek Feedback: Reach out to local friends, colleagues, or mentors for feedback. They can provide valuable insights and guidance on how to rectify the mistake and avoid similar pitfalls in the future. Constructive feedback is a valuable resource for cultural learning.

Apologize and Make Amends: Don't hesitate to apologize sincerely if your mistake has caused offense or discomfort. Demonstrating genuine remorse and a commitment to understanding and respecting the local culture can go a long way in repairing relationships.

Continue Learning: Treat each mistake as a learning opportunity. Study the cultural aspects that led to the error: language, etiquette, or social norms. Consider taking cultural sensitivity workshops or language classes to enhance your knowledge and skills.

Challenge Assumptions: Be aware of your own cultural biases and preconceived notions. Challenge these assumptions and actively seek to understand the perspectives and values of the host culture. Engage in conversations, ask questions, and listen attentively to local insights.

Embrace a Growth Mindset: Cultivate a growth mindset, which involves believing that your abilities and intelligence can be developed through dedication and hard work. Embracing this mindset can help you view mistakes as opportunities for improvement rather than failures.

Stay Resilient: Don't let fear of making mistakes deter you from engaging in cultural experiences. Mistakes are a natural part of the process, and resilience is vital to overcoming challenges and continuing your cultural learning journey.

Keep a Cultural Journal: Consider maintaining a journal documenting your cultural experiences, including successes and mistakes. Writing about your experiences allows reflection and helps track your progress over time.

Share Your Experiences: Share your cultural learning journey with others, whether through blogs, social media, or conversations with friends and family back home. Sharing your experiences can inspire others to embark on similar journeys and reinforce your learning.

Remember that cultural competence is an ongoing process, and perfection is not the goal. By approaching mistakes as opportunities for growth, you enhance your cultural skills and develop a deeper understanding and appreciation of the host culture.

Plan Your Time

Planning your time abroad when studying in a foreign country is of paramount importance for a successful and enriching experience.

Effective planning ensures you maximize your opportunities abroad, learn, and overcome potential challenges.

- **Academic Success:** Planning your educational path is essential—research and select courses that align with your academic goals and requirements. Make sure your chosen courses fit into your degree program and will contribute to your overall education. Review the course schedule, prerequisites, and credit transfer policies to avoid academic setbacks.

- **Cultural Immersion:** Planning allows you to allocate time for cultural immersion. Consider participating in local events, festivals, and cultural activities. Planning cultural experiences enhances your understanding of the host culture and offers opportunities for meaningful interactions with locals.

- **Language Learning:** Plan for language learning if your host country has a different language. Enroll in language courses, practice with locals, and allocate dedicated study time. Language skills not only facilitate communication but also deepen your cultural understanding.

- **Travel Exploration:** Studying abroad often includes exploring nearby regions and countries. Create a travel bucket list and a budget for your trips. Plan your vacations wisely to balance academic responsibilities with leisure travel.

- **Professional Development:** If your study abroad program allows for internships or part-time work, plan your career development. Seek opportunities that align with your field of study or career goals. Networking and gaining practical experience can be invaluable for your future.

- **Health and Well-being:** Prioritize your health and well-being by researching healthcare facilities, insurance coverage, and any specific health considerations in your host country. Make a checklist of necessary vaccinations or medications and ensure you can access medical support if needed.

- **Budget Management:** Develop a comprehensive budget that includes tuition, living expenses, travel, and leisure activities—factor in currency exchange rates and fluctuations. Monitor your expenses regularly and adjust your spending to stay within your budget.
- **Accommodation Arrangements:** Plan your accommodation well in advance. Consider whether you'll live in university dorms, homestays, or off-campus housing. Secure accommodations that are safe, convenient, and align with your preferences.
- **Cultural Adaptation:** Recognize that adapting to a new culture can be challenging—plan for cultural adaptation by studying local customs, norms, and etiquette. Be open-minded and patient, and seek support from fellow international students, mentors, or cultural orientation programs.
- **Emergency Preparedness:** Develop a contingency plan for emergencies. Familiarize yourself with local emergency numbers, embassy contacts, and evacuation procedures. Keep important documents, such as passports and visas, securely.
- **Time Management:** Cultivate practical time management skills. Create a weekly schedule that balances classes, study time, cultural activities, and personal relaxation. Time management is essential for maintaining a healthy work-life balance.
- **Personal Goals:** Reflect on your personal goals for the study abroad experience. Whether building self-confidence, expanding your worldview, or developing independence, having clear personal objectives can guide your decisions and actions.
- **Stay Connected:** Maintain communication with family and friends back home. Please share your experiences and seek their support. Staying connected can provide stability and emotional well-being during your time abroad.

Effective planning lets you make the most of this transformative experience, fostering personal and professional development while creating lasting memories. Remember that flexibility is also key; while planning is essential, being open to unexpected opportunities and challenges can further enhance your study abroad journey.

Be A Part Of Your Host Country's Cultural Milieu

Becoming an integral part of your host country's cultural milieu is an enriching experience that fully immerses you in the local way of life. It can deepen your understanding of the culture, foster meaningful connections, and create lasting memories. Here are some strategies that can help:

Learn the Language: Language is a powerful tool for cultural integration. Dedicate time to learning the local language or at least some basic phrases. Language skills enhance your ability to communicate with locals and participate in daily life.

Live with Locals: Whenever possible, opt for living arrangements that involve locals, such as homestays or shared housing. Living with locals exposes you to their daily routines, customs, and traditions.

Participate in Cultural Activities: Attend local cultural events, festivals, and celebrations. These gatherings offer a window into the local culture, with opportunities to witness traditional practices, music, dance, and cuisine.

Join Community Groups: Many countries have local community groups or clubs centered around various interests, hobbies, or causes. Joining these groups allows you to interact with locals who share your passions and can provide valuable cultural insights.

Explore Local Cuisine: Food is a universal language. Experiment with local dishes street food, and dine at local restaurants. Exploring the local cuisine is a delicious way to connect with the culture.

Travel Within the Country: Take advantage of your time abroad to explore different regions within your host country. Each region often has its own unique customs, dialects, and traditions.

Attend Local Classes or Workshops: Enroll in classes or workshops that teach traditional skills or arts, such as dance, music, crafts, or cooking. Learning these skills from local experts can provide a deeper connection to the culture.

Volunteer: Engage in volunteer work or community service projects. Contributing to the local community fosters a sense of belonging and allows you to interact with locals while making a positive impact.

For example, Australia is known for its outdoor lifestyle. Engage in activities like surfing, hiking, or barbecues at the beach. These are not only great ways to meet Australians but also to embrace their love for the outdoors. You can learn about and respect the Indigenous culture of Australia. Attend cultural events, visit Indigenous heritage sites, and consider engaging in Indigenous cultural immersion programs if available.

In the Netherlands, you can embrace the Dutch passion for cycling. Rent a bicycle and explore the city and countryside. Cycling is an efficient mode of transportation and a fantastic way to experience Dutch daily life. You can also participate in King's Day (Koningsdag), the national holiday celebrating the Dutch monarchy. Wear orange, join in the festivities, and experience the vibrant street markets, music, and cultural celebrations.

Germany is renowned for its festivals, from Oktoberfest to Christmas markets. Attend these events to taste traditional foods, enjoy live music, and interact with locals who are proud of their cultural heritage. While many Germans speak English, learning German enhances your cultural integration. Consider enrolling in language courses or practicing your German with locals.

In all cases, approach cultural integration with an open mind, respect for local customs, and a willingness to adapt. Building relationships with locals and actively participating in cultural activities will deepen your understanding of the culture and leave you with a sense of belonging and memorable experiences that last a lifetime.

Work Opportunities

Exploring work opportunities in other countries can be an exciting and enriching experience, offering you a chance to gain international work experience, build your professional network, and immerse yourself in a different culture.

Internships: Interning abroad is a popular choice for students and recent graduates. It allows you to gain hands-on experience in your field of study, learn about international work practices, and enhance your resume. Many countries offer internships in various industries, including business, finance, technology, and hospitality.

Teaching English: Teaching English as a foreign language (TEFL) is a common way for native English speakers to work abroad. You can find opportunities to teach English in schools, language institutes, or private tutoring. This experience provides a source of income and allows you to engage with local communities and enhance your teaching skills.

Working Holiday Visas: Some countries, like Australia, New Zealand, Canada, and certain European nations, offer working holiday visas to young adults from eligible countries. These visas allow you to work and travel in the country for a specified period, typically one year. It's an excellent opportunity to fund your travels while gaining work experience.

Au Pair Programs: Au pair programs enable you to live with a host family in a foreign country and provide childcare in exchange for room, board, and a stipend. It's a cultural exchange opportunity that allows you to immerse yourself in a family's daily life and learn about their culture.

Research Positions: If you're pursuing graduate or postgraduate studies, consider research opportunities abroad. Collaborating with international research institutions or universities can broaden your academic horizons and contribute to your educational and career growth.

Freelancing and Remote Work: Many professionals can work from anywhere with the rise of remote work and the gig economy. Consider freelancing or remote work opportunities that allow you to work for international clients while residing in a foreign country.

Working for Multinational Companies: Some multinational companies hire employees to work in their overseas branches or offices. You may find job opportunities within these global organizations if you have specialized skills or qualifications.

Entrepreneurship: Launching a business or startup in a foreign country can be an entrepreneurial adventure. Research the local business environment, regulations, and market trends to determine if there are opportunities to start your venture.

Volunteer Work: While not typically paid, volunteer work abroad allows you to contribute to meaningful causes and gain valuable experience. Many volunteer programs provide room and board in exchange for your service.

Part-Time Jobs: Depending on the country's regulations and your visa status, you may be eligible for part-time work opportunities, such as working in restaurants, retail, or the service industry. Part-time jobs can help cover living expenses while abroad.

When exploring work opportunities in other countries, it's crucial to research visa requirements, work permits, and legal regulations. Additionally, consider your goals, skills, and interests to determine which work opportunity aligns best with your personal and professional aspirations.

Chapter 28:

Seeking Immigration While Studying Abroad

Acquiring a Permanent Residency (PR) while you're a student abroad is a significant opportunity that provides numerous benefits and opens up new horizons. While the rules and eligibility criteria vary from one country to another, many host countries offer pathways for international students to obtain PR status.

Pathways to PR for Students Abroad

One of the notable pathways for international students to secure a Permanent Residency (PR) while studying abroad is through post-study work visas. Countries such as Canada, Australia, and the United Kingdom offer this opportunity. After completing their studies, international students are granted a specific duration of post-graduation work experience. This experience can serve as a crucial stepping stone toward acquiring PR, as it allows students to establish themselves in the host country and build a professional network.

Skilled migration programs are another route that many countries offer to attract highly skilled individuals, including recent graduates. These programs often assess eligibility based on age, education, work experience, and language proficiency. Qualifying through skilled migration programs can lead to PR, enabling international students to contribute to the host country's workforce and society.

Family sponsorship provides an alternative path to PR for students abroad. If an international student has family members who are already PR holders or citizens of the host country, they may have the option to be sponsored for PR. The feasibility of family sponsorship varies depending on the host country's immigration policies, but it can be a viable option for those with eligible family members.

Some countries, like Canada, have Provincial Nominee Programs (PNPs) that permit provinces and territories to nominate individuals for PR based on their specific labor market and economic needs. Studying in a particular province can enhance your chances of being nominated under these programs. By actively participating in the local workforce or demonstrating a commitment to that province, students can align themselves with the requirements for nomination.

Entrepreneurial and investor programs present an intriguing path to PR in certain countries, such as the United States. The EB-5 Investor Visa program allows individuals to obtain PR by investing in job-creating businesses. Similarly, other nations offer entrepreneur visa programs, making PR attainable for those interested in starting or investing in businesses that can contribute to the local economy.

Benefits of PR While Studying Abroad

Attaining PR status while studying abroad brings forth a multitude of advantages. It offers a long-term stay in the host country, enabling students to establish a sense of stability and security during their academic pursuits. This permanence fosters a deeper connection to the local culture, allowing students to immerse themselves more thoroughly in their studies and the broader community.

PR often comes with enhanced work flexibility expanding job opportunities. Holders of PR status can typically seek full-time positions across various sectors without the constraints imposed on international students, who often have limitations on the number of hours they can work. This work flexibility can be particularly beneficial in gaining valuable professional experience.

Access to government-funded healthcare and education is another critical benefit of PR status. In many host countries, PR holders can take advantage of national healthcare systems and benefit from reduced tuition fees at educational institutions. This alleviates the financial burden on students and their families, making education and healthcare more accessible.

PR status often serves as a stepping stone to citizenship, granting individuals the same rights as native-born citizens. This includes the right to vote and participate in the country's political processes, allowing PR holders to shape their adopted home's future actively.

One of the practical benefits of PR is the elimination of the need for visa renewals. International students often face the administrative challenges of renewing student visas or work permits. However, once PR status is obtained, individuals no longer need to navigate this cumbersome process, as PR provides ongoing legal residency.

Social benefits, such as unemployment benefits and pension plans, are typically extended to PR holders. These government programs offer financial security and support in times of need, ensuring a safety net for individuals during their time in the host country.

PR status facilitates international travel. PR holders often enjoy simplified international travel arrangements, as they can re-enter the host country without a visa. This flexibility streamlines travel plans and makes exploring other countries easier for leisure and professional purposes.

PR can simplify family reunification. It can make it easier to sponsor family members for PR or facilitate their entry into the host country through family reunification programs. This brings families together, fostering a more inclusive and supportive environment for students who choose to study abroad.

It's important to note that acquiring PR while studying abroad is typically a multi-step process that may require meeting specific criteria, such as language proficiency, work experience, and regional considerations. Consulting with an immigration expert or seeking guidance from your host institution's international office can be valuable in navigating the PR application process.

Benefits Of Relocating To Another Country

Relocating to another country is a life-changing decision that brings about a multitude of benefits and opportunities. Whether you're pursuing education, a career, or a new way of life, the advantages of living in a foreign country are numerous and can profoundly impact personal growth, cultural understanding, and professional development.

One of the most significant benefits of relocating to another country is the opportunity for personal growth and self-discovery. Living in a new environment challenges you to adapt and develop valuable skills such as adaptability, problem-solving, and independence. You're exposed to different cultures, customs, and ways of thinking, which broaden your perspective and enhance your global awareness. This intercultural competence and cooperation enrich your personal life and become an invaluable asset in an increasingly interconnected world.

Cultural immersion is another compelling advantage. Relocating to another country allows you to experience a culture in its natural context. You'll have the chance to engage with locals, participate in cultural activities, and even learn a new language. This deep cultural understanding fosters empathy and tolerance, making you more open-minded and accepting of diverse perspectives. It's an immersive experience that enriches your life in profound ways.

On a professional level, relocating to another country can significantly enhance your career prospects. It offers the opportunity to gain international work experience, which is increasingly valuable in today's global job market. You'll build a diverse professional network and acquire unique skills that set you apart from your peers. Many employers value candidates with international experience for their adaptability, cross-cultural communication skills, and ability to navigate diverse work environments.

Moving to another country can open doors to unique educational opportunities. You may have access to prestigious universities, specialized programs, or research facilities that align with your academic and career goals. It's a chance to receive an education that can be transformative and provide a competitive edge in your field.

From a lifestyle perspective, relocating to another country often introduces you to a higher quality of life. Many countries offer excellent healthcare, safety, and social services, contributing to well-being. Exploring different cuisines, landscapes, and recreational activities can be exhilarating. You'll create lasting memories and gain a deeper appreciation for the world's diversity.

Family and personal relationships also benefit from relocation. Living in a foreign country can bring family members closer as they navigate challenges and adventures together. It can also allow children to learn in diverse educational settings and develop strong cross-cultural skills early on

Moving to a new place can be challenging. You have to handle paperwork, learn a new language and might miss home a lot. But these difficult times can make you stronger and help you grow as a person. You'll learn to overcome obstacles, a valuable life skill.

How To Acquire PR

Obtaining a Permanent Residency (PR) in different countries can be a complex process, with each nation having its own rules and eligibility criteria. Here are some common ways to acquire PR in various countries.

Canada

Canada is known for its welcoming immigration policies. The Express Entry system is one of the most popular routes to Canadian PR. It's a points-based system that evaluates candidates based on age, education, work experience, and language proficiency. Successful candidates receive an Invitation to Apply (ITA) for PR. Completing a Canadian post-secondary program can provide additional points in the Express Entry system, making it a favored choice for international students seeking PR.

Australia

Australia offers a similar point-based immigration system called the General Skilled Migration (GSM) program. To qualify for PR, candidates must submit an Expression of Interest (EOI) and receive an invitation to apply for a skilled visa. After completing their studies, international students can transition to the Temporary Graduate Visa (Subclass 485). This visa allows them to gain work experience in Australia and can be a stepping stone to PR through the skilled migration pathway.

United States

Acquiring PR in the United States is typically based on employment or family sponsorship. Employment-based PR categories include the EB-2 and EB-3 visas, which require sponsorship from a U.S. employer. Some international students may secure PR through Optional Practical Training (OPT) or the H-1B visa, which can eventually lead to employment-based PR. Additionally, family members who are U.S. citizens or permanent residents can sponsor their foreign relatives for family-based PR.

United Kingdom

The UK offers several routes to PR, such as the Tier 2 (General) work visa, which can lead to Indefinite Leave to Remain (ILR) after five years of continuous residence. After completing their studies, international students can apply for the Tier 2 (General) visa upon securing a job in the UK. The Ancestry visa is also available to those with a grandparent born in the UK and can lead to ILR.

New Zealand

New Zealand offers a points-based system for PR through the Skilled Migrant Category (SMC). To qualify, candidates must meet health and character requirements and score a minimum number of points based on factors like age, work experience, and qualifications. Completing a recognized New Zealand qualification can earn additional points, making it a beneficial pathway for international students.

European Union (EU)

The EU offers a variety of immigration programs in its member countries, with differing rules and requirements. For instance, in countries like Germany, students who graduate with a recognized degree and secure a job offer may be eligible for the EU Blue Card, a pathway to PR. In other EU countries, investment-based visas, family reunification, or long-term residency permits may be options for acquiring PR.

China

China's PR policies are often tied to employment and family connections. In many cases, foreigners who have worked and resided in China for a specified period and have paid taxes can apply for PR. Family members of Chinese citizens or PR holders may also be eligible for family-based PR.

United Arab Emirates (UAE)

The UAE offers several routes to PR, including investment-based visas, skilled worker visas, and long-term residency permits. These options cater to different categories of applicants, including entrepreneurs, professionals, and retirees, making securing PR possible for individuals from various backgrounds.

These are just a few examples of the diverse pathways to PR in different countries. Each country's immigration system is unique, and navigating the process can be complex. It's essential to consult with immigration experts, legal professionals, or the respective country's immigration authorities to understand the specific requirements and procedures for acquiring PR in your chosen destination.

Chapter 29:

Using Study Abroad Experience for Global Growth in Home Country

Studying abroad can be a transformative experience that enriches your life while abroad and equips you with a wide range of skills and perspectives that can contribute to your success upon returning home.

Using Your Study Abroad Experience At Home

Living in a foreign country exposes you to diverse cultures, traditions, and perspectives. This firsthand experience enhances your cultural awareness and sensitivity, which can be invaluable when interacting with a diverse community back home. You become more adept at understanding and respecting individual differences, contributing to harmonious relationships and effective communication.

If you studied in a country where a language other than your native tongue is spoken, you likely acquired or improved your language skills. Being bilingual or multilingual can open doors to various professional opportunities, enabling you to communicate with a broader range of people and access international job markets. Your enhanced language proficiency can be a competitive advantage in many industries.

A study abroad experience offers a global perspective that goes beyond textbooks. It gives you a deeper understanding of international affairs, economics, and politics. This global perspective can be valuable in a wide range of fields, from international business to diplomacy, as it allows you to assess and adapt to global trends and issues.

Living abroad requires a high level of independence and adaptability. You learn to manage your daily life, navigate unfamiliar environments, and problem-solve in various situations. These skills can be transferred to your career and personal life, making you more resourceful and capable of confidently tackling challenges.

Your study abroad experience likely led to a diverse network of international contacts. These connections can be leveraged for both personal and professional growth. Networking with individuals from various backgrounds can introduce you to new opportunities, whether it's international business partnerships, collaborations, or cross-cultural projects.

Overcoming the challenges and uncertainties of living in a foreign country cultivates resilience. You learn to adapt, persevere, and remain resilient in the face of adversity. This skill can help you handle stress and uncertainty, making you more resilient and determined in your home country.

Soft skills, such as cross-cultural communication, adaptability, and empathy, are highly sought after by employers. Your study abroad experience equips you with these skills, making you a more attractive candidate in the job market. Soft skills play a crucial role in leadership, teamwork, and problem-solving, all contributing to professional success.

Conquering the challenges of living in a foreign country fosters a sense of self-confidence. You'll become more self-assured in your abilities to handle unfamiliar situations and communicate effectively, whether personally or professionally. This self-confidence can propel you forward in pursuing your goals.

Exposure to different cultures and ways of thinking sparks creativity and innovation. You gain fresh perspectives and insights that can inspire creative problem-solving and innovative ideas. Whether you're an entrepreneur, an artist, or a professional in any field, these qualities can drive success.

Incorporating your study abroad experience into your personal and professional life back home can be a powerful catalyst for success. It provides a unique set of skills, perspectives, and characteristics that enhance your competitiveness, enrich your personal life, and contribute to a fulfilling and prosperous future in your home country.

Building Your Skills

Building on the experience and skills acquired during your study abroad journey is a key aspect of maximizing the benefits of this transformative experience.

Start by reflecting on your study abroad experience. What were the most significant lessons you learned, both personally and professionally? Identify the skills you acquired, the challenges you overcame, and the areas where you experienced personal growth. This self-assessment will help you understand your strengths and areas for improvement.

Maintain the cultural sensitivity and awareness you gained abroad. Be open to understanding and appreciating diverse perspectives in your home country. Seek opportunities to engage with people from different backgrounds through cultural events, volunteering, or multicultural groups.

If you improve your language skills while abroad, continue to use them in your daily life. Join language clubs, find language exchange partners, or seek opportunities to tutor others. Bilingual or multilingual abilities are assets that can be harnessed in various personal and professional contexts.

Nurture the relationships you established abroad. Stay in touch with the friends you made and the international contacts you acquired. These connections can offer insights, networking opportunities, and even potential collaborations in the future.

Seek out international activities and events in your home country. Attend cultural festivals, international conferences, or seminars that align with your interests. These gatherings can provide a sense of continuity with your global experiences.

If you developed a passion for international affairs, consider pursuing a career with an international focus. Options include diplomacy, international business, global development, and NGOs. Your study abroad experience can be valuable in securing positions in these fields.

Consider continuing your education with a postgraduate degree related to international studies or a subject you became passionate about during your time abroad. Higher education can provide you with specialized knowledge and enhance your career prospects.

Participate in global organizations, such as international chambers of commerce, cultural associations, or international nonprofits. These groups offer opportunities to engage with like-minded individuals, collaborate on projects, and advocate for global causes.

Seek mentorship from individuals who have successfully built on their study abroad experiences. They can offer guidance and insights on translating your experiences into meaningful career paths.

Use your newfound skills and experiences to give back to your community. Consider volunteering, sharing your experiences with local schools, or participating in community development projects. Your global perspective can be an asset in creating positive change at home.

Commit to lifelong learning. Continue to explore new cultures, languages, and perspectives. Whether through books, online courses, or travel, maintain an inquisitive and open mindset.

The skills and experiences gained during your study abroad journey are valuable assets that can continue to shape your life and career long after your return.

Global Growth In Your Home Country

Bringing global growth to your home country is an ambitious and impactful endeavor that harnesses the knowledge, skills, and experiences gained during your study abroad journey. This endeavor can contribute to your nation's development, promote cross-cultural understanding, and create opportunities for economic, social, and intellectual advancement.

International business and trade are the primary avenues to bring global growth to your home country. You can use your connections and insights from your study abroad experience to establish partnerships, export products, or expand markets. Fostering international trade relations can stimulate economic growth and create job opportunities, making a tangible impact on your country's prosperity.

Promoting cultural exchange and education is a powerful means to bring global growth. Collaborate with educational institutions to facilitate student exchange programs, language learning initiatives, and intercultural workshops. By creating platforms for cultural exchange, you enhance cross-cultural understanding and equip the next generation with the global perspectives needed to thrive in an interconnected world.

If you've acquired an entrepreneurial spirit during your study abroad experience, consider launching your startup or business venture in your home country. Leveraging international insights and skills can lead to innovative solutions that address local or global challenges. These entrepreneurial endeavors can stimulate economic growth and job creation while fostering innovation.

Forge international partnerships between your home country and the nation where you studied. Collaborative agreements in various fields, such as research, education, and technology, can drive economic and intellectual growth. International partnerships open doors to shared resources, knowledge transfer, and collaborative projects that benefit both countries.

Use your understanding of global cultures to promote cultural exchange and appreciation in your home country. Organize cultural festivals, exhibitions, and events celebrating the world's diversity. These initiatives enrich your society and create economic opportunities for local artisans and artists.

Engage in diplomacy and advocacy efforts that promote global growth. Advocate for policies that encourage international cooperation and support sustainable development. Diplomacy and advocacy can influence international relations and foster positive change in trade, climate, and social justice.

If your study abroad experience ignited a passion for philanthropy and social impact, consider establishing or contributing to initiatives that address global challenges. By directing resources toward healthcare, education, environmental conservation, or social welfare projects, you can create lasting positive change in your home country and beyond.

Share your experiences and knowledge with individuals in your home country, especially those interested in international careers, cross-cultural communication, or global issues. Mentorship and knowledge sharing can empower the next generation of global leaders and professionals.

Collaborate with research institutions, think tanks, and organizations to conduct international research and innovation projects. These initiatives can yield insights, solutions, and intellectual advancements that contribute to global growth, particularly in technology, health, and environmental sustainability.

Engage in public awareness campaigns and educational initiatives to increase your home country's understanding of international affairs, global challenges, and opportunities. You contribute to informed decision-making and active participation in global issues by raising awareness and fostering a global mindset.

The skills, experiences, and connections you've gained during your study abroad journey position you as a catalyst for change and progress. By actively engaging in initiatives like these, you can contribute to your home country's development, promote cross-cultural understanding, and help create a more interconnected and prosperous world.

Chapter 30:
Wrapping It All Up

Moving on, I will offer a CTA to my clients to visit my website, book a consultation, or send me an email.

This book was your guide to the world of international education. It explored the idea of studying abroad and its many life-changing benefits. We delved into topics like moving to a new country, exposure to different cultures, pursuing a quality education, and the people you met along the way.

We also discussed how this journey could boost your career and personal growth, no matter what stage of education you were in - from school students to undergraduates and graduate-level scholars. You learned how studying abroad could help you gain new skills, expand your network, and experience various teaching styles.

We even helped you find ways to fund your adventure. This book aims to simplify the complexities of international education and provide you with the knowledge and inspiration you need to take the life-changing step of studying abroad. It was a journey that could make your life easier, more enriching, and transformative.

Here's a simple overview of everything we covered.

Moving Abroad and Making Your Life Easy

Moving abroad is a significant life decision that offers a multitude of opportunities and experiences. It's a transformative experience that can simplify your life in ways you may not have considered. When contemplating this transition, you need to consider various aspects such as the process of migration, the benefits of studying abroad, the exposure it provides, the quality education available, the introduction to new cultures and people, the career prospects, and the immense personal growth that comes with it.

How Can One Migrate Abroad?

Migrating abroad can be a complex process that requires careful planning and execution. It involves obtaining the necessary visas, permits, and documentation, understanding immigration laws, and potentially dealing with language and cultural barriers. Additionally, exploring options like work visas, student visas, and skilled worker programs is crucial, depending on your goals. Research, preparation, and possibly enlisting the help of immigration experts or agencies can make the process smoother and ensure a successful migration.

Benefits of Studying Abroad

Studying abroad offers a myriad of benefits. Beyond academic qualifications, it immerses oneself in a new culture, fostering cultural sensitivity and a global perspective. Exposure to diverse teaching styles and learning environments enhances critical thinking and adaptability. The experience of studying abroad can also lead to lifelong friendships, a broader network, and personal growth, which are invaluable for personal and professional development.

The Exposure That Comes

One of the most significant advantages of studying abroad is the exposure it offers. Living in a foreign country exposes you to new traditions, customs, and a way of life entirely different from what you are accustomed to. This cultural immersion encourages an open-minded attitude, a deeper understanding of global issues, and the ability to appreciate and respect different perspectives.

Quality Education

Quality education is a cornerstone of studying abroad. Many renowned universities and institutions worldwide offer world-class education, and this exposure can significantly impact your academic and professional future. It allows you to gain access to top-notch faculty, research opportunities, and state-of-the-art facilities that can shape your knowledge and skills for years to come.

New Culture, New People

Moving abroad is not just about academics but also about embracing a new culture and connecting with new people. Interacting with individuals from different backgrounds enriches your life in countless ways. It broadens your horizons and helps you develop a global mindset. The friendships formed during this time can be lasting and may open doors to exciting opportunities and experiences.

Career Opportunities

Studying abroad can significantly enhance your career prospects. Employers often value candidates with international exposure, as they tend to possess a broader skill set, adaptability, and a deeper understanding of global markets. It also provides access to internships, co-op programs, and networking opportunities that can jumpstart your career.

Personal Growth

Personal growth is an inherent part of studying abroad. Living in a foreign country forces you to step out of your comfort zone, face new challenges, and develop self-reliance and resilience. This personal growth can positively affect your self-confidence, problem-solving abilities, and overall life skills.

Benefits of Studying Abroad for School Students

For school students, studying abroad can be an enriching experience that goes beyond the classroom. It encourages independence and self-sufficiency from a young age. School students have the opportunity to engage with diverse cultures and gain a global perspective that can shape their future academic and career choices.

Benefits of Studying Abroad for Undergraduate Students

Undergraduate students can benefit immensely from studying abroad. Beyond acquiring academic qualifications, they can learn new skills in and out of the classroom. This period is ideal for personal growth, self-discovery, and building a global network that can provide lifelong support.

How Graduate-Level Students Can Benefit from Studying Abroad

Graduate-level students can take advantage of the advanced education and specialized knowledge available abroad. They gain exposure to different teaching styles, research opportunities, and the potential for a great career. Additionally, graduate-level studies can boost their confidence, encouraging independent thinking and research skills.

How To Choose the Right Program for You

Selecting the right program is crucial for a successful overseas education experience. Factors to consider include your academic and career goals, personal interests, and preferred destination. Additionally, you should consider the program type (e.g., exchange, degree, language course) that suits your needs and budget, as well as the duration and cultural fit of the program.

How to Find the Right Kind of Funding Sources

Financing your education abroad can be challenging, but numerous funding sources are available. These sources include scholarships, grants, part-time work opportunities, and student loans. Finding the proper funding that matches your financial situation and educational needs is crucial to making your dream of studying abroad a reality.

Study Abroad Checklist for the USA

This chapter provides a comprehensive checklist for students aspiring to study in the United States. It includes information on visa requirements, university selection, financial planning, standardized tests, application processes, and considerations for cultural adjustment. The USA is one of the top destinations for international students, and this chapter offers vital guidance to ensure a smooth transition and successful academic journey.

Study Abroad Checklist for Canada

For those considering Canada as their study destination, this chapter outlines the necessary steps for a successful experience. It covers visa applications, choosing the right Canadian institution, financial preparation, English proficiency requirements, and other practical advice. Canada is known for its diverse and inclusive education system, and this checklist will help prospective students make the most of their time in the country.

Study Abroad Checklist for the UK

Studying in the United Kingdom is a dream for many international students. This chapter offers insights into the UK's educational landscape, visa processes, university selections, scholarships, and considerations for adapting to the British culture. It's a valuable resource for those looking to embark on their academic journey in the UK.

Study Abroad Checklist for Australia

Australia is renowned for its high-quality education and vibrant lifestyle. In this chapter, students will find guidance on student visa applications, selecting the right Australian institution, financial planning, English language requirements, and tips for embracing the Australian way of life. The checklist equips aspiring students with valuable information to make their experience in Australia a success.

Study Abroad Checklist for Singapore

Singapore is an emerging hub for international education, and this chapter delves into the intricacies of studying in this dynamic city-state. It covers student pass applications, university choices, financial considerations, and cultural tips to adapt to Singapore's cosmopolitan environment. The checklist aids students in preparing for a unique educational journey in Singapore.

Study Abroad Checklist for Dubai

The United Arab Emirates, particularly Dubai, has become a prominent destination for international students. This chapter offers valuable insights into visa requirements, university options, financial planning, and adjusting to life in the UAE. As Dubai grows as an education hub, this checklist is a valuable tool for students considering this location.

Study Abroad Checklist for Denmark

Denmark is known for its high-quality education and quality of life. This chapter outlines visa procedures, choosing Danish institutions, financial aspects, and tips for cultural integration. It provides an essential guide for students exploring the Scandinavian education system.

Study Abroad Checklist for the Netherlands

The Netherlands is a popular destination for international students, and this chapter offers guidance on Dutch student visas, university choices, financial planning, and tips for embracing the Dutch culture. It serves as a roadmap for students considering the vibrant academic landscape of the Netherlands.

Study Abroad Checklist for Sweden

Sweden's education system is known for its innovation and quality. This chapter explores the steps to study in Sweden, including visa applications, university selections, financial aspects, and adapting to Swedish life and culture. It's an invaluable resource for those considering higher education in Sweden.

Study Abroad Checklist for Switzerland

Switzerland is synonymous with excellence in education. This chapter offers insights into Swiss student visas, university choices, financial planning, and recommendations for thriving in the Swiss academic environment. Aspiring students can rely on this checklist for a successful study abroad experience in Switzerland.

The chapters in the book provide in-depth checklists and guidance for studying in other countries, including Russia, India, Germany, Italy, Spain, France, Hungary, China, Ireland, New Zealand, and Japan. Additionally, the book addresses crucial topics like ensuring your safety abroad, immersing yourself in the host culture, making the most of your time abroad, and seeking immigration opportunities while studying abroad. Each chapter is a valuable resource for students planning to pursue their education in these respective countries, offering a holistic view of the considerations and steps needed for a successful international academic experience.

You can schedule a consultation call with our experts if you have further inquiries.

We help you move abroad by giving you the necessary advice and information. Trust us to guide you every step of the way!

We know much about immigration laws and can give you personalized advice on moving abroad. We'll help you find the best way to move to your dream country. Want to learn more? Visit our website!

https://kumardirect.kartra.com/calendar/Ashwin

Lastly, you can always drop an email at ashwin@kumardirect.com

Made in the USA
Coppell, TX
16 January 2025

44504048R00174